kindness now

A 28-DAY GUIDE TO LIVING WITH
AUTHENTICITY, INTENTION,
AND COMPASSION

———

AMANDA GILBERT

FOREWORD BY TRUDY GOODMAN, PhD

SHAMBHALA

Shambhala Publications, Inc.
2129 13th Street
Boulder, Colorado 80302
www.shambhala.com

Cover art: Allison Meierding
Cover design: Allison Meierding
Interior design: Kate Huber-Parker

9 8 7 6 5 4 3 2 1

Printed in the United States of America

♻ Shambhala Publications makes every effort to print on recycled paper.
For more information please visit www.shambhala.com.
Shambhala Publications is distributed worldwide by Penguin Random
House, Inc., and its subsidiaries.

Library of Congress Cataloging-in-Publication Data
Names: Gilbert, Amanda (Meditation teacher) author.
Title: Kindness now: a 28-day guide to living with authenticity,
    intention, and compassion / Amanda Gilbert.
Description: Boulder: Shambhala, 2021.
Identifiers: LCCN 2020045729 | ISBN 9781611809015 (trade paperback) |
ISBN 9781645471530 (Five Below edition; trade paperback)
Subjects: LCSH: Meditation.
Classification: LCC BL627 .G55 2021 | DDC 294.3/4435—dc23
LC record available at https://lccn.loc.gov/2020045729

FOR VICKI

———

who showed me the
limitless potential
of the human heart

CONTENTS

FOREWORD

TRUDY GOODMAN, PhD

This book, *Kindness Now*, is inviting you to embark on one of the most exciting adventures of your lifetime. Imagine discovering that you are in possession of a hidden treasure, a valuable trust fund containing an abundant supply of love, compassion, joy, and serenity. Imagine that you can access your inner trust fund through meditation exercises, practical tools to help you face whatever happens in your life with more confidence, strength, and kindness. And imagine learning that your unruly mind can be tamed by your very own kind heart. Wouldn't that be amazing? This is the promise of *Kindness Now*: in twenty-eight days of practice, you can rock your world, tilting your whole life in a new direction.

Through a skillful weaving of Buddhist and Western psychology, Amanda Gilbert gently guides you through "the hard work of heart work." She shows you how to outfit a mobile home for your heart so you can navigate this life more smoothly, with gratitude and ease. You can take your time and go at your own pace. Amanda shows the way through her skillful weaving of honest personal experience and ancient wisdom. You can travel secure in the knowledge that you're being guided by an expert in these time-honored teachings that have helped millions of people for thousands of years.

Beautifully written, *Kindness Now* is based on mindfulness meditation. It is a thorough and generous articulation of the *brahma-viha*ras, the "divine abodes"—the beautiful places the heart can dwell in peace and happiness. The brahma-viharas are lovingkindness, genuine compassion, all-inclusive joy, and courageous equanimity, and they work like magic. After fifty years of my own study and practice of these teachings, I'm struck by a great mix of enthusiasm, humility, and patience with which Amanda hands you a whole set of keys to unlock the doors to your own trustworthy, kind heart. Over and over again, she reminds us all that these qualities are innate. They are planted in the human psyche, seeds simply waiting to be seen and watered. You are holding a portable garden in your hands, one that can live in your heart's mobile home. Best of all, this book takes you there.

Read this, treasure this, keep this in your heart.

INTRODUCTION

Be kind. It shakes the world.
—Cleo Wade

I've come to understand there are two places where we meet our full unfiltered humanity. One is in the journey between heartbreak and healing. And the other is where we deal with this inevitable process—on the meditation cushion. The latter is a place where humans have gone to metabolize our most unearthing and life-affirming experiences while being in the uncharted terrain of discovering what it means to feel whole, complete, and at ease in our own skin.

I've also come to learn that the very same qualities that make us human, from our ability to love someone thoroughly to spontaneously smiling at someone as they walk by on the street, also enable us to make it from the rumbles of setbacks, breakups, and great losses to rebuilding ourselves in the aftermath. This is the quality of kindness. Kindness is what the human heart is made of. It gives us the wisdom, strength, and perseverance to face our most vulnerable and difficult life moments. And it guides us in uncovering the bottomless depths of our love, our compassion, and our most genuine dreams and intentions. Through kindness we realize healing is possible, feeling good is possible, and meeting our full authentic selves is possible.

And it is the very quality that enables us to make it through one meditation session, one messy human moment at a time.

Kindness is now about to get the spotlight it deserves in your life, and I'm so happy we get to walk down this path of understanding and discovering together. The very fact that you are holding this book in your hands means you are ready to find out what the teachings of kindness have in store for you. Let me tell you, I am confident that these pages and twenty-eight days of practice will rock your world. More so, I am confident that learning how to meet yourself and the world with kindness now will be the exact inner resource you have been looking for. To put it simply, kindness heals. And I bow to your heart's wisdom for guiding you here to train your heart and mind in becoming an even more loving, understanding, and compassionate human being.

the ways of kindness

Whether we realize it or not, we all live on kindness. We rely on the good-heartedness of complete strangers who give us directions when we are lost or hold the elevator door so we can make it to that meeting just on time. I've depended on kindness too many times to keep track of. In fact, kindness has been the very gift that has supported me through my biggest life-altering mistakes, mega-moments of disappointment, and all the small unfoldings of life's daily prickliness and pain. We learn the way of kindness by being on the receiving end of countless selfless acts, caring concern, and bighearted compassion—such as when a friend calls to lend an empathetic ear and words of encouragement, or when a coworker senses we're not quite ourself that day and stops to make sure we're okay.

Another way we come to know kindness is by learning how to extend to ourselves this same good-heartedness and care we receive from others. Really, kindness is the way of love and the foundation of self-love. It is how each and every one of us heals from all that breaks our heart, and it is how we come to know the very fabric of the human heart itself—our own true nature; our trustworthy, wise, loving self; what Buddhism calls our "basic goodness." I like to think of basic goodness as our authentic essence coupled with the innate kindness we already possess within us. This innate kindness automatically ignites when you accidentally cut your finger or scrape your knee and a few minutes later you find yourself carefully placing a bandage in gentle protection over the newly acquired wound. Or when you tend to your own basic needs—from making sure your financial life is in check, to feeding your body right, to finding a safe place to rest or call home.

Kindness is even expressed through self-care. Those daily rituals of going to the gym, painting, creating, or—yes, you bet—meditating are all ways we learn to be kind and loving toward ourselves. Don't worry if self-kindness feels really far away right now or if when you read the word *self-care* your eyes glaze over with guilt at the very thought of taking time for yourself. In *Kindness Now* I'll show you how your innate kindness and foundation of self-love are right here, already pumping away in your veins just as your true, genuine, authentic self is right here, just waiting to be uncovered.

Through opening our hearts to receive kindness from others and by bravely learning how to be kind to ourselves, instinctually we also become adept in the third way of kindness: being kind to others. Whether responding to a friend's cry for help or to the racial, gender, and social inequities we see being overtly displayed in our own neighborhood and city, or offering a helping hand to a total stranger we notice needing assistance, kindness carries us and reminds us of our common humanity. It reminds us just how much our self-love and self-worth flourish when we share our basic good-heartedness and care with others while healing their hearts and reminding them of humanity's capacity to live kindly.

Kindness unites us. It connects us from birth to death, where in two of our most vulnerable and defenseless moments, as we transition in and out of this world, 100 percent reliant on the fundamental care of the human heart. Kindness is how we channel this basic good-heartedness and care, our empathy, and our shared humanity beyond personal ideologies, belief systems, political views, and interests. Understanding that kindness is the very matter weaving together all of our existence, we can allow our own undertakings of kindness to be our conviction of love and stepping into our authentic, wise, compassionate self. I know it is how I really began to live a life where I felt whole, unbroken, purposeful, and fully alive. This is what kindness does—it points us to what is really important, to what really matters, and to what is meaningful. It brings us home to the love that we already are.

My purpose in writing this book is to share with you a set of meditation teachings that has been used for centuries by people just like you and me, who are ready to heed the heart's call and arrive home to the loving-kindness already within. You are someone who knows there is something more, or something deeper. You have the intuition in your heart and gut, or the inkling within the marrow of your bones, that meditation holds the key to your own healing, recovery, and journey back to wholeness, happiness, and health. In truth, this *is* what meditation does. It waits for you until you are ready, and no matter why you show up at its doorstep, you soon discover how it does indeed hold the answers your heart has been looking for. In other words, it points you to what is real—the kindness, love, and inspiration we all need to keep greeting another morning, and to help others along the way realize they too are not alone in wanting to uncover a sense of home and belonging and to rest in the natural goodness of their own heart and mind.

Real meditation holds within it the innate teachings on love, presence, and the healing transformation of kindness. Being kind is both a way of being and a choice we make in the present moment, just like mindfulness is. The Buddha gave us a great insight into how meditation is actually supposed to work. He taught that we must become "skilled in goodness" in order to know the "path of peace."[1] This goodness he is referring to is the heart of a real supportive and flourishing meditation practice. In order to truly gain insight and peace in the present moment, we must learn to skillfully meet what is here with the qualities of the heart: a nonjudgmental loving-kindness, the clarity of compassion, the delight of genuine happiness and true joy, and the wisdom and balance that comes from equanimity. Known in Buddhism as the *brahma-viharas*, or the heart practices of mindfulness meditation, these are the teachings of transformation that, when applied to our modern life, will actually lead us to the real change and shifts we've been searching for.

This is the promise of not only the brahma-viharas but also *Kindness Now*. As a meditation teacher, lecturer of mindfulness, and longtime meditator, I am committed to sharing with you what ended up being a big turning point during the course of my seventeen years of meditation practice and the very teachings that provide relief and meaning to thousands of people I teach each year. When I applied authentic kindness to my meditation practice, I finally found the heart medicine I needed to feel whole again and to meet my real authenticity. Kindness has shown me how to live through tragedy, trauma, post-traumatic stress disorder (PTSD), anxiety, and many self-limiting beliefs to being unapologetically wholeheartedly free and at ease in my own skin. Now I get to see this very same life-defining moment take place in those I share meditation with. The times I have heard my students say "I feel like I'm finally meditating for the first time" or "Oh, this is what was missing . . . being kind to myself" are numberless. Especially if you have labeled yourself as "not a good meditator," or you feel as though you "just can't sit down to meditate at all," kindness is the missing ingredient that will allow you to actually meditate, my friend. And if you are a longtime meditator, these practices of the heart will rock your world, not only deepening and transforming your meditation practice but also changing how you interact in every single relationship and life circumstance in which you find yourself. The brahma-viharas are the way of love, the path of the heart, and so often the missing ingredient to a successful daily meditation practice.

the heart practices

The brahma-viharas have several names. These qualities of the heart are also referred to as the "four sublime states," the "four limitless qualities," the "four boundless qualities," the "four immeasurables," "the four faces of love," or the "four heavenly and divine abodes." If you are thinking this all sounds amazing and "Where do I sign up for this?"—you're not alone. When I first heard these traditional names for the heart practices, I instantly thought, "Yes, please. I definitely want to rest in boundless love and kindness. Show me the way, I'm there." Traditionally taught together, loving-kindness (*metta*), compassion (*karuna*), appreciative joy (*mudita*) and equanimity (*upekkha*) are what make up the brahma-viharas—*brahma* meaning "heavenly" or "best," and *vihara* meaning "dwelling" or "home." These teachings are a systematic road map for training the heart to rest in its true nature, which is free, unobstructed love. Together, they create a formula for building an unconditional loving abode for the heart and mind to dwell in, and a place of real refuge where you can gain clarity and solace from what is bringing you out of alignment or causing you difficulty, hardship, and pain. For modern meditators, it is where we learn to meet what we become aware of in meditation—the judgy thoughts, the prickly envy, the debilitating unworthiness, the grief of heartbreak, or the fear of not knowing whether we can pay our bills—with an empathetic feeling of honest understanding, authentic kindness, and wise compassion. This is where we learn how to assimilate and compost the garbage and the good in our lives. You can even think of kindness as the very ingredient that starts, sustains, and finishes the composting process—turning the raw material of difficulty and decay into fertile ground for something beautiful to eventually bloom in. And this is all done by bringing kindness to the here and now.

I was first introduced to the heart qualities on a pivotal day during my ninth year of having a meditation practice. After an initial period of following our breath in meditation, the long-time Buddhist meditation teacher, with the gentlest presence and voice, interjected with the guidance, "And now begin to send yourself the following wishes of loving-kindness: May I be happy. May I be healthy. May I be free from suffering. May I live with ease." These words were completely and utterly new to me. I had primarily meditated upon objects of attention such as mantras or the breath and had never heard these exact phrases before. As I listened to our meditation leader recite these phrases with such care in his voice, I let the phrases and sayings wash over me. Even though at first they felt a little alien and uncomfortable, I could just sense their innate goodness. Beneath the awkward discomfort of telling myself, for the first time, to be happy and then realizing that I really did want to be happy, deep down I knew these phrases were good for me and most undeniably they felt good in my heart. They were filled with warm, rather sweet sentiments that felt more like gentle whispers of thoughtful intentions. This day ended up being not only the day I opened the door into a whole new world of the heart but also the very first time I learned to meet myself with genuine kindness, thus starting a whole new chapter in my life and practice.

how to use this book

This book is a training for how to uncover meaning, truth, purpose, and healing through learning how to be kind. It is the road home to our fundamental wholeness and innate capacity to love ourselves through all the failures, disappointments, and upheavals. It is what I've wanted during my most disorienting and inconceivable times: a place to go that I could trust wholeheartedly, a judgment-free friend I could be embraced by, a mentor and guide willing to hold my brokenness or reignite inspiration in my life and on the meditation cushion, a home where I could access unconditional loving acceptance so I could rest and reset in order to begin again.

I wrote this book to be your daily practice companion and meditation buddy for the next twenty-eight days. Think of this book as a full-on heart download on the ways of kindness, love, joy, and compassion and a deeper invitation to becoming steadfast and consistent with your practice. If you show up and do the work, you will notice your heart and mind transform. You will gain the psychological insights, wisdom, and deeper self-awareness you are searching for. It is also a guide to go deeper—a place to let things fall apart with the trust and faith there is someone and something to support you in putting the pieces back together again. And yes, this all can happen through the lens of adding a little more kindness and compassion to your practice and life, and it doesn't have to look perfect, as you'll soon discover.

Over the next four weeks, you will learn and practice the heart qualities by growing your understanding of each, week by week. You will be following a well-traversed path through the landscape of the four foundations of the heart. Each week I will introduce you to one of the brahma-viharas with a daily teaching, a guided meditation, and modern metta mantras (loving-kindness phrases for all four heart qualities) meant to become your new best friend to carry around with you during the day. We're going to aim for a few pages of reading and then ten to twenty minutes of meditation followed by mindful journaling and practice reflections.

- Week 1: Metta—Loving-kindness. This week guides you in teachings on metta where you will learn the powerful yet subtle ways you can meet yourself and others with kindness. You will understand what is blocking you from self-love and the ability to wish yourself authentic happiness and kindness, and how to extend metta toward others in your life, including your most difficult people!
- Week 2: Karuna—Compassion. This week guides you into the healing world of compassion and the many different facets of learning to meet yourself and others with greater wisdom and understanding. You will learn the heart principles of self-compassion, forgiveness, unconditional love, right action, and dedicating the merit of your meditation.
- Week 3: Mudita—Appreciative Joy. This week guides you to your true experience of genuine happiness and authenticity. You will uncover the deeper blocks and underpinnings of

the ego while learning that real love and connection come from the generosity of an expanded heart. You'll come to realize that celebrating the happiness of others is a direct pathway to experiencing happiness in your life.

· Week 4: Upekkha—Equanimity. This week guides you to your new baseline of being. It will cement the divine abode you have been building over the past three weeks of heart-based practice. You will learn how equanimity is the biggest contributing factor to living a meaningful life and feeling fulfilled, at peace, and content while giving you the capacity to live in today's world with an open heart.

PREPARING THE GROUND

Early on in my meditation path, I heard some really helpful advice on how to continue growing a meditation practice. The advice was this: If you just spend the next ten years of your life listening to other people talk about meditation, then that will only get you so far down the meditation road. On the other hand, if you just sit and meditate for the next ten years of your life, that too will only get you so far down the road of growing a real meditation practice. The point? You need a little bit of both. You need the conceptual understanding of how the practice works, what signposts to look for, and what to expect as you traverse this well-traveled path. And you need direct experience in the practice itself. No one else can meditate for you. You have to show up, do the work, and apply the principles of practice yourself. This is how you get far down the path of practice. This is how you make great progress on the road of meditation.

I still refer back to this fundamental truth. This approach shaped how I continued to seek teachings on meditation and my daily practice. To keep walking forward on the path of awakening the heart and mind, you need to keep learning and steadily applying what you are learning about the practice. The first three chapters of this book are meant to prepare you for the twenty-eight days of deepened practice ahead. Think of them as your extra-helpful framework in understanding how the compassionate and loving heart leads you home to your authenticity through intentionally living these practices each and every day. Plus, you can confidently roll into our twenty-eight days of practice with a solid understanding of the type of meditation and inner work that is in store for you.

- Chapter 1, "A Call from the Heart," will guide you in finding your true authentic nature and home within through kindness.
- Chapter 2, "A New Way of Living," will teach you how to live your life with great purpose and intention by getting to know the powerful intersection of the mind and heart.
- Chapter 3, "Real Change," shows you that real transformation and healing are possible by approaching change as a practice of compassion.

You can read the first three chapters over the course of a week or weekend before beginning the twenty-eight days of heart practice. Or skip directly to the four weeks of practice and dive right in on page 29.

A PRACTICE JOURNAL

Every day, after each meditation, there will be reflection questions for you to contemplate and take with you into the day. These reflection questions are also awesome journal prompts, carefully and scientifically constructed to help you learn more about each of the heart qualities, go deeper into each of the practices, and take your self-insight and practice to a whole new level. My suggestion is to have a journal next to you when you are meditating, then pick up the journal and write out your practice insights as you reflect on the daily mindful inquiries and reflection questions. You'll also notice more journaling guidance in Week 1 compared to the following three weeks, as by then you will have learned how to approach your post-meditation reflection questions.

LIVING FROM THE HEART

A key part of our work together over the next month will center around uprooting your conditioning of fear, judgment, and any blocks you have to giving or receiving unconditional kindness and love. You'll end each meditation session with an in-the-moment actionable practice. These mobile heart practices are ways to extend your learning and insights of the brahma-viharas into any present moment and to live each day from love.

be ready. be committed.

Throughout your twenty-eight days of exploring the landscape of your heart and mind, inevitably strong emotions and experiences will come up. Not every meditation teacher will tell you this, but I think it is helpful to keep the following in mind: Though this practice is for everyone—every single human being on the planet—taking the next step in meditation is not for the faint of heart. This journey requires courage, commitment, and a real readiness to meet yourself with openness, humility, and love.

Given the terrain you are embarking on—training for a heart that is boundless, limitless, and unconditional (no big deal, right?)—you too will have to be unconditional with your-self. Regardless of how you feel, whether it is convenient or inconvenient, hard or easy, you can choose to open your heart in the face of both happiness and discomfort. When you bump up against your past regrets, pain, or mistakes, you will need to be brave enough to stay with it and keep going down the path. Try making meditation one of your new daily nonnegotiables. Know that encountering discomfort and difficult thoughts is actually a good sign. Trust me. It means you are moving through layers of thoughts and emotions that are ready to be released and healed, which will only happen through the commitment and willingness to keep showing up for your very own heart and mind.

Are you ready? Let's begin.

kindness now

1

a call from the heart

WE ARE ALL DRAWN to meditation for a reason. It's a primal calling that's innate and intrinsic to every single human being regardless of one's upbringing or background. This longing for truth and happiness defines so much of our lives. You'll find it nestled within every decision and detail in each chapter of your life story. It's there as you grow older and search for success, stability, and a way to carve out your own little plot of space in this life. It is woven into all of your most fundamental needs and desires for acceptance, belonging, partnership, and a safe place to rest your head and heart at the end of the day.

Whether we know it consciously or not, we are all looking for a way to find the authentic truth of who we are and a home where we can be exactly *who* we are in the world. The soft lure of meditation's song is one the heart knows all too well. It is the call for love, the hymn of real happiness, and the boundless joy of finding the truth of who we are and feeling at home within ourselves no matter where we are or who we are with. Beneath the mind's reasoning or the magnetism of what's trending in medicine or modern wellness is the timeless yearning to arrive home to the unbiased love and unconditional resilience in the heart of the present moment. This is what you are being pulled to—the natural state of unconditional loving awareness found already within you. And the way you get there is through uncovering your own good-hearted nature, a kindness as ancient and intrinsic as the genetic sequences that make up your DNA. I am deeply grateful to have found this place of authenticity within my own heart and mind, as it has shown me how to align myself with love instead of fear, judgment, self-hatred, and attack pretty much every day of my life since I stepped on the path of my own meditation journey.

I meditated for the first time when I was in high school. I was seventeen years old and finishing my last semester at a wilderness-based home school in West Virginia. This was not your traditional type of school experience. My peers and I were there because we basically couldn't make normal high school situations work for us. We were either struggling in school or finding ourselves getting into trouble of some kind. Even as a teenager I had pretty much become completely disillusioned by school and my life. I felt alone even though I was friends with everyone regardless of what social clique they were in. I found no meaning or happiness in any of my school studies other than some brief moments during art class. I walked around with a heavy feeling of overall dissatisfaction, so I would act out by being late to class or not going to school on some days. Every school or class I went to felt empty—void of anything real, trustworthy, or comfortable to me. I could not find anywhere I felt completely at ease or free to be me. Looking back on the adolescent angst I used to feel, I can so strongly see now just how much I wanted to feel at home in myself and in my life. All of my unhealthy behaviors at the time were unskillful attempts at reaching outward for deeper understandings of how life works and wanting to feel self-love, self-acceptance, and peace.

The nontraditional high school I found myself in during my senior year was run by Native American elders, local Appalachians, and a principal who had spent years studying the ancient wisdom traditions of South American indigenous cultures. As you might imagine, embedded in the school's curriculum were some unconventional lessons. Alongside reading about algebra and finishing my last credit of science I needed to graduate, we began each morning in a circle, being guided to close our eyes and turn our attention within. Once we had stopped fidgeting or resisting the request to be quiet and introspective, we were asked to place our attention on the breath and find our "sense of center" and "true north." After a few minutes of having our attention on the breath, we were then asked "to forgive ourselves and let go of the past" and to get "clear and focused" for the day. These mornings—all circled up in a hut deep within the rolling hills of the Appalachian Mountains, with our hiking boots laced up and schoolbooks out for the day—were the very first moments I ever felt a real sense of home and feeling at ease within myself. There was a deep peace that seemed to stem from inside of me, and I remember feeling a special presence that was both within me and all around me. This special presence was full of tenderness, strength, warmth, and boundless love. It made me feel whole and happy all at the same time. This was my actual first experience with mindfulness and metta (loving-kindness). By being asked to place my attention in the present moment, I encountered a presence of unconditional and limitless love.

These initial moments of meditation significantly shaped the trajectory of my life. The longtime Buddhist meditation teacher Sharon Salzberg says, "We realize through our practice that a loving heart is our natural home, and through our practice we can always find our way home."[2] In many ways, ever since I came into contact with the feeling of being at home in my own body and heart, and first meeting my "true north," I've been committed to finding my way back to that familiar yet boundless place within me, even if only for a split second in the midst of my daily meditation practice. The taste of feeling whole and held in the field of love that lives in any given present moment has kept me coming back to my practice with utter blind faith yet total trust and confidence for over seventeen years.

The call or hold meditation has over my heart is one of the truest feelings I've ever come to know. The little home of my own true nature I touch down in every day has become the through line of my life over the past decade or more, and has allowed me the greatest gift of all—to keep following my heart's call. This little heart home has moved with me in and out of too many apartments to recall, through more cities across the United States than I care to admit, and most importantly through the different phases and chapters of my life. From total backcountry wilderness night skies to the center of cities that seasoned me with the culture and societal learnings I didn't receive growing up amid the cornfields of small-town Ohio, it's been with me. All of which has led me to this very moment, writing to you now to say, if anything, I wish you the honest courage and willingness to heed your own heart's call and build your mobile home inside your unconditional loving heart.

The call from your heart is the same call to find your genuine home burrowed within each breath and within your radiant, loving, natural heart-state filled with endless kindness and compassion. The unconditional home of love found through my meditation practice, so intrinsic and trustworthy, has held me when no one else was there to wrap their arms around me and give me comfort or provide soothing words. My loving awareness has watched me unravel, fall apart, cry, and wail through some of life's most inconceivable moments, including trauma, breakups, financial despair, loss, and betrayal. When I entrusted my brokenness, flagrant mistakes, and flaws to this bedrock of love, I answered my heart's call to come home to the truth of the present moment and to be brave enough to forge ahead in discovering the truth of who I am in this moment, right here and now.

This is how the heart practices bring you home. They are abodes built by your own consciousness holding the very key to your unique inner peace and your heart's call to the medicine of your authenticity. Over the course of the next twenty-eight days, you will learn how to practice with these four faces of love, meant to bring you and your heart back home to who you really are, and create a clear enough channel of self-awareness infused with loving-kindness to overcome self-doubt, lack of self-confidence, and the prevalent experience of feeling like an imposter in your own life. The brahma-viharas will teach you the way out of feeling like a fraud, fearful to really let anyone in and see you for who you really are; or feeling broken beyond repair, as if your wings will always be clipped by your wound-edness and inability to feel whole.

It is said that the dharma (truth), the Sanskrit word for the Buddha's teachings, is like finding refuge under the shade of a canopy-rich tree after traveling weary and parched, oppressed by the heat of a desert sun. Under the coolness of the shade, with your back resting against the knobby bark of a tree trunk strong enough to withstand the aging seasons of weather and the windy tests of time, your tired body is able to let go into the invisible city of roots below. Finally you have found a place to rest and unravel. Finally you are able to let your mind and heart unwind and unfurl, under the protection and safety from sun or storms or any weather pattern in life's journey. The Buddha's teachings on finding the truth within our hearts give us the means to finally be able to see ourselves clearly, free from our conditioning, negative self-talk, skewed body image, or all the nasty stories we tell ourselves on repeat yet would never even whisper anything of resemblance to someone else.

finding your truth

I often think back to the countless times I've tried to find a semblance of home, safety, truth, and love anywhere other than within myself. For years, my mode of making decisions was by seeking advice and feedback from everyone else—literally anyone. First I would call one of my parents or run options by my boyfriend, then I'd call my sister or brother, followed by a text to one of my best girlfriends. On really indecisive days I would even try to interject my current circumstance along with the available choices into conversation with the innocent coffee shop barista or a stranger who unfortunately (for them) said hi to me on the train. My decisions and autonomy were all run through the mill of others' opinions, ideas, judgments, and perceptions. It wasn't until I was able to bring this doubt-laden lack of self-trust and low self-worth to the forefront of my conscious awareness that I was able to heal it. And the real healing only began after recognizing with mindfulness my ingrained patterns playing out over and over and then choosing instead to work with these self-insights with a heavy heart-dose of kindness and self-compassion.

Similarly, the quest for ways to define who we know ourselves to be starts within our toy-strewn childhood playrooms, the bus rides to grade school in the rain, and even in the selection of our first Halloween costumes. We look for remnants of our self-reflection everywhere. When our parents or caregivers tell us we are special or beautiful, we adopt these beliefs to be true until someone tells us otherwise: a third-grade classmate points out our freckles while waiting in line for ice cream in the school cafeteria; a middle-school classmate names the jiggle in our thighs. I can recall during both of these moments the abrupt awakening of learning something about myself I hadn't known before. Both of these remarks shaped my self-identity at the time: "I am a girl with freckles on my face and kickball-strong thighs; I'm not as small or attractive as some of the other girls in my grade." Our identity becomes built upon praise from our teachers, parents, and friends, or the shame from not measuring up to their expectations of us or the expectations we place upon ourselves. We can go along this way for years, looking for a feeling of familiarity, belonging, and acceptance in just about anyone who shows care for us. Our life becomes the story of this search, while what we're really looking for is the answer to who we actually are.

The brahma-viharas offer us a way out of this common confusion and a place of undeniable freedom. It was so freeing for me to return my sense of self-reference from others back to my own confident, self-assured home within myself. The fragmentation I was always feeling lessened. And owning my truth—even the not-so-wise choices and decisions and all the seemingly unlikeable traits—has saved my life and sanity. The heart practices share the dharma of how each of us can find our radiant, whole, and authentic self, also known as our buddha nature. In order to be yourself, you first must know yourself and uncover the truth of who you are, by understanding the dharma of your own heart.

Zen Master Huang Po, an early influential luminary of Zen Buddhism, describes it this way:

The heart is the source, the pure buddha nature that is inherent in all of us.

When you have within yourself a deep insight into this, you immediately realize that all that you need is there in perfection and in abundance, and nothing is at all wanting or lacking in you.[3]

As you move through the upcoming month of practice, I want to share with you the following set of principles to help remind you that what you are doing is uncovering *what is already here inside of you* and what is already perfectly here in abundance. Your authentic abode of buddha nature is a lot closer than you think. It is so close. It is as familiar as the sound of your breath or the way you know your heart to beat within your chest. The heart is the source, and all we are setting out to do is to help you answer the heart's primal call to come home to your own true nature—your buddha nature, the shining source and truth of who you are.

four steps for answering the call no matter what

During your practice this month, without a doubt you will encounter well-known universal obstacles and individual hindrances to answering the heart's call, such as fear, apprehension, resistance, self-flagellation, or doubt. I encourage you to lean on the following four steps as a way to prepare yourself for these inevitable run-ins with your ego, your inner critic, and all the conditioning that may still be running the show and keeping you from resting in the heart of who you really are. The moment you find yourself resisting your meditation practice on that day or wanting to avert or hide from seeing and loving your authenticity, I want you to call to mind these principles meant to guide you back home to the love within your heart.

STEP 1: CALL OUT THE OBSTACLE

Notice and call out the obstacle at play and bring your mindfulness to it so you can see it clearly. As you'll learn in chapter 2 as well as during each week of *Kindness Now*, mindfulness and metta go hand in hand. Mindfulness, the ability to see what is happening clearly from one moment to the next, will show you precisely where to apply your heart practice. When any aversion or doubt comes up this month, take a mindful step back and ask yourself, "What's actually true for me right now? Is fear here? Judgment? Jealousy? Comparison? Confusion? Doubt? Lack? Or any other old habit patterns from my conditioning and past?" Actualizing your authenticity through the heart will take clarity and courage, so to the best of your ability, call out the resistance and obstacles that you feel, look them square in the eye, and name them with your awareness.

STEP 2: MOVE OUT OF RESISTANCE
AND INTO ACCEPTANCE

All obstacles to resting in your true buddha nature are forms of fear-laden resistance to showing up in your full unique expression of *you*. The quickest way to work with this resistance, once you have named it as you did in step 1, is to accept it. You can even silently say to your resistance at any time, "I see you. I hear you. I know that you are here. I accept you." If you give this a try right now, you may notice an immediate alleviation of shame or guilt to any feeling of resistance or hindrance to stepping into the truth of who you are. Acceptance is a powerful ally to actualizing your authenticity. It moves you one step closer to true inner freedom.

STEP 3: ANSWER WITH THE HEART

From Day 1 onward, you will be able to access the precise heart qualities that any situation and scenario asks for. For instance, if you are feeling an old familiar pattern of closing down to your own authenticity or feeling fearful of how you will be perceived by others, you can immediately respond with compassion once you've named and accepted the obstacle at play. Week by week during the next month, you will focus on one loving abode of the heart at a time. My suggestion is to stick with the exact heart quality you are working with during that week and keep adding as you go along. For example, by Week 3 you will have learned loving-kindness, compassion, and appreciative joy but not yet equanimity. So on Week 3, when an obstacle to feeling at home in your own heart comes up, call upon metta, karuna, or mudita. Then after Week 4 you can add upekkha to your inner resources of the heart as well. The purpose of this is for you to be fully heart-based at the end of the twenty-eight days, with a confident understanding of each unique heart quality as you progress through each week.

STEP 4: RETURN TO LOVE

Once you've called out, accepted, and answered from the heart, step 4 is to completely and utterly return. What are you returning to? Your authentic heart, your genuine sense of home within, the feeling of being safe and protected in the sanctuary of your heart, and your own basic goodness and buddha nature—the unconditional loving awareness that you are.

When practiced over and over, these four steps become more natural and simply a part of who you are. This method is a way for you to keep uncovering your true self even in the face of difficulty and doubt, fear or uncertainty. After learning the brahma-viharas, I now know to pause and practice these four steps in the face of self-hatred, self-doubt, or wanting to throw myself into the home of another person or relationship. On learning the way of the heart, I often say to my students, "This is going to be full of hard work! Yet here, the hard work is really the heart work."

Each principle shared above always brings me back home to my authentic energy, my core essence, and the organic unfolding awareness I am in any given moment. I promise they will do the same for you. The heart qualities serve as your way to stay on track and become who you are and who you want to be. My commitment to you in the pages of *Kindness Now* is to keep reminding you to be brave enough to call out any obstacle in your path, to meet resistance with wisdom and grace, to learn how to pull from your inner resources already available to you, and to choose love. And keep choosing love, over and over.

2

a new way of living

EVERYTHING IN YOUR life begins with intention. Even having the intention to discover your true authenticity, to become more self-aware and create a home out of your heart, starts out with a deep intention and aspiration to do so. Living with intention is precisely *where* the heart and the mind meet. This meeting ground of the mind and heart is where your authentic expression and greatest aspirations flow from, rooted in big life-changing love.

When you contemplate your intentions, which we will do together in this chapter, you will discover just how powerful the precise mixture of mind and heart is. Your mindfulness will hold the vision for you; it will see what it is you want and what is of greatest benefit for everyone around you. Within the mind resides your innermost wisdom—what Buddhists call "wise view." Your heart holds the deep unconditional love and compassion you will be training for by studying and living the brahma-viharas over the next twenty-eight days. This is what *Kindness Now* is all about—learning to live your life between the divine balance of wisdom and love and making your home base of being and living a dynamic expression of these two forces.

where the heart and the mind meet

In Tibetan Buddhism, the word *chitta*, which is translated as both "mind" *and* "heart," encompasses this intersection of the mind and the heart. Chitta is heart-minded consciousness, the meeting of mindfulness and metta practice, and the very place you will learn to set your intentions from. Here, each thought stems from your buddha nature and each gesture and act comes from a place of wise love.

For many years before I began teaching meditation, I spent time working at one of the world's top health psychology laboratories, helping to conduct clinical research on meditation. I was fascinated to understand the exact mechanics of what made meditation so potent and life-changing. I ran nationally funded research on behalf of my esteemed mentor Dr. Elissa Epel, a leading researcher on telomeres, cell aging and stress resilience, when our colleague Dr. Clifford Saron, a longtime Buddhist meditator and one of the world's top scientists in contemplative research, shared a story with me about chitta, which forever impacted my own understanding of just how intertwined our minds and hearts really are.

Early on in his neuroscience research career, Dr. Saron was collaborating with longtime friends and fellow neuroscientists Dr. Richard Davidson and Dr. Francisco Varela. Saron, Davidson, and Varela's personal love of meditation and their own quest for truth through Buddhist-inspired teachings greatly informed their career paths. So much so they found themselves part of a group of Western scientists traveling to the foothills of the Himalayas in India to conduct research with yogis living in rural mountain stone retreat huts and to host dialogues with His Holiness the 14th Dalai Lama on where Western science and Tibetan Buddhism may share common ground.

In one of his early missions, Saron and his team lugged their brain measuring equipment to McLeod Ganj, the small hill station where His Holiness the Dalai Lama lives, with the aim to study the effects of meditation on the brains of longtime monks living in one of the oldest known monasteries. Many of their study participants, some having been ordained in the monasteries as young as seven years old, had been practicing meditation their entire lives. What ensued completely encapsulates the essence of chitta.

As Saron tells the story, the researchers were giving an EEG demonstration to a group of student monks at the Institute of Buddhist Dialectics. Varela himself was sitting in the front of the room, with the EEG electrode cap on and was providing brain waves for the demonstration, when one of the student monks paused and asked the scientists, "Why are you putting the recording cap on Francisco's head when everyone knows the mind is here?" pointing to the center of his chest. The entire room erupted in chuckles and roaring laughter as the question was translated to the full group. This ended up being a real moment where Western scientists and practitioners where able to understand just how heart-centered the mind is viewed in traditional practice settings and teachings. To longtime practicing Buddhist monks there isn't a distinction between the mind and the heart; to them, both live in the center heart space of the chest.

I invite you to pause and reflect for a moment: What would it be like to live from a mind and a heart that are viewed as one? How would this chitta approach inform your daily choices and decisions and, even, their outcomes? If you're thinking is based from the compass of your heart's values and its authentic guidance, then every thought, choice, action, and intention would be based in the heart's innate qualities of love, kindness, nonharm, and empathy. This is how we set our intentions from a mind whose home is rooted in the heart.

intentions keep you close to home

Setting intentions is a way to stay aligned with your heart and come back home to your genuine nature. Most importantly, they keep you close to home, or at the very least going in the direction you consciously want to be going in. More so, they are the means to manifesting your most authentic heart-based self. Without living intentionally, you won't be able to let your full potential be realized in the boundless way in which it could. The brahma-viharas serve as a road map in this way, showing you how to live from your wisest of intentions, the ones infused with big-hearted love.

As mentioned in the introduction, I want you to be psyched and prepared to fully commit to your meditation practice and sacred heart time each day. Being intentional about your practice means creating the time, space, permission, and support to do the inner work and begin to form a strong connection with your chitta—that meeting place of your mind's wisdom and your heart's boundless love. The wise mind will guide you in contemplating an intentional routine, schedule, and structure; and the heart will give you the kindness, inspiration, and bravery required to consciously show up to your practice each and every day. Knowing your intentions and spending time consciously constructing your daily practice and daily life with chitta will help you seamlessly integrate this way of living into your life. I promise that the short practice I have for you next will strongly support you in remaining heart-centered, even if you are a classic overthinker or overachiever, or if you feel like you can't get quiet enough to hear what your heart and mind really want.

living your intentions

Becoming who you are depends on how you live each day. When you aren't clear enough with your intentions or your motivations, your reason for meditation can become half-hearted—more of a "let me check this off the to-do list" type of vibe that largely misses the deeper heart benefits of the practice. Or it simply may not happen at all. There is a Vedic approach to meditating each day, or building a morning sadhana (spiritual practice), that I found very helpful. Meditate first thing in the morning for twenty to thirty minutes—have it be literally the first thing you do after brushing your teeth and getting a glass of water or a small sip of coffee or tea. This routine was the very spark I needed to ignite my own daily practice. There I was, getting up hours before the start of my day just so I could have enough time to meditate uninterrupted for up to an hour! Equally, though, when I dug a little deeper, what was also bubbling below the surface of my newly emerging daily meditation habit was my *why*—my deepest intention for why I would motivate myself to get up at 5:00 a.m. instead of sleeping in for the extra hour.

There were also days when I would be peering through the sides of my eyes at my meditation cushion, thinking, "Really? I'm going to meditate when I'm feeling this sleepy, sad, or stressed? When I'm already wondering how on earth I'm going to get everything done on my to-do list today? Really? I'm still going to sit down and meditate feeling like this?" The deeper reason, beyond just the routine of daily meditation, was because my heart was healing. I was feeling happier and more alive and with the world instead of unconsciously moving through my day. My heart was beginning to feel porous and open again. And I so looked forward to showing up as who I was becoming and getting the opportunity to share my openheartedness with the people I saw and worked with every day. The awareness of my deeper why helped me through any resistance I might have been feeling and to wholeheartedly make meditation a part of my daily routine.

In this way, the following practice is meant to bring you clarity on your deepest intentions—how you want to share your heart with the world and what structure will make you feel the most supported and inspired to make the next twenty-eight days the start of a new life chapter for you.

intention-setting contemplation

This may be your first practice journal entry! If so, welcome home to your heart practice! Or if you have already started with the twenty-eight days of brahma-vihara practice, go ahead and turn to a fresh page for the following contemplations on living from the heart and from your wisest, deepest of intentions.

I invite you to take a deep breath, place a hand on your heart, read each contemplation, and then spend a few minutes in stillness allowing your awareness to explore the intentions and answers that come through. Follow this chitta contemplation practice with writing down your intentions and new insights for showing up to your practice, creating an intentional routine and structure, and being a heart-based human being sharing your unique gifts of practice with the world.

Ready, take a deep breath, pick up your pen, and begin.

REFLECTION QUESTION 1: Who do you want to be?
REFLECTION QUESTION 2: How do you personally and glob-
ally want to live?

REFLECTION QUESTION 3: What characteristics or qualities would you like to plant in your heart? In other words,
what heart qualities are you aware of right now that you
want to cultivate?

REFLECTION QUESTION 4: What structures and routines
would be supportive for you in becoming heart-based? I
encourage you to write down a daily meditation routine
with as much detail as possible. When will you meditate
with your *Kindness Now* practice? How much time will
you dedicate to your kindness practices? Where will you
practice? What does your daily sadhana look like? How is
it bookended—for example, with lemon water? breakfast?
movement? your workday?

When you are finished with these four reflections, pause
for a moment and thank your inner wisdom and heart. You
can even silently say, "Thank you, my wise heart, for always
guiding me home."

———

When your intentions are from both the mind and the heart,
your way of being in the world is an expression of living your
love. Ensuring to practice each day, even on the not-so-convenient
ones, only makes you a stronger and brighter channel for the
kindness and heart the world so needs right now.

And, as you'll discover in chapter 3, you will attain the
transformation and real change you seek by letting your way
of relating to the world around you flow between wisdom and
love. Real change *is* possible by committing to transforming
your suffering through your daily practice and letting your
heart lead with compassion. Remember, becoming who you are

is directly dependent on what you do each day. So in the very same way, real change comes from you showing up to your truth, your wounds, your healing, and your own limitless love, regardless of any obstacles that get in your way. And chapter 3 will show you how.

3

real change

IF THERE IS ANYTHING I know to be true, it is this: real change is possible. And within this very same breath, as I write these words to you, I also know there is a second part to this truth: real change is possible *and* it is a constant practice, much like meditation. When we set out to meditate, or to start any new endeavor that we have locked our eyes and heart on, there are two important ingredients to approaching real change as a practice: choice and compassion.

Change is a choice, and, in many ways, real deep-rooted change requires intentional upkeep, perseverance, and a ton of heart when we get off track, lose momentum, or sidestep any of our greatest aspirations and intentions all together. Every heartfelt wish, change, and new habit will meet the inevitable human dichotomy of success and failure, working and definitely not working, triumphant joy and apathetic non-follow-through. What I know from my experience of practicing my authentic expression and my nearest and dearest heart-based truth and intentions is this: real change is a practice. It will ask you to choose it moment by moment, sometimes a hundred times a day, so how you approach the practice of real change is key.

And this is where compassion comes in. Compassion—with its forgiving, understanding grace and strength—will enable you to keep choosing what you want with clarity and conviction. Compassion will give you a way to return home to your inner compass of authentic intentions and support you in turning your resistance, moments of failure, and obstacles into purpose and vehicles for connection.

Compassion, the second of the brahma-viharas, will be your entire focus for Week 2 in your upcoming twenty-eight days of heart practice. Compassion is an essential ingredient to cultivating the type of inner and outer change you want to see within yourself and the world because compassion makes imperfection and failure okay. Compassion draws from your heart's innate loving nature the part of you that cheerleads any underdog or up-and-coming heroine or hero in their journey of becoming the best version of themselves. It is your natural ability to accompany someone—yourself or someone else—as they climb their mountain; teeter toward the top; become overcome with hail, thunder, and torrential rain; and rejoice as they muster the energy and courage to begin the traversing and ascension process again.

Real change can be staggeringly messy, often coming on the heels of imperfection, the exposure of your unknown shortcomings and blind spots; through unexpected detours, personal breakdowns, or life situations that alter reality as you once understood it. Born into this human experience is the intrinsic moment-to-moment constancy of change, so for our purposes during *Kindness Now*, it is essential to create the right conditions for real change. Genuine inner change doesn't stand a chance against the preexisting forces of self-judgment or the ingrained habits of self-betrayal. Real transformation comes only when it is safe enough to do so, when it is free from condemnation, judgment, or the destruction of mistrust. The seeds of real change can only take hold when there is a kindhearted, spacious, accepting, loving approach to the choice and a practice in which to take root. It knows when you are willing and ready to meet the practice and constant choosing with compassion. This, my dear friend, is what the magic of real change is made of. I can't think of a more noble pursuit worthy of your time, stamina, and commitment. To greet your intentions for real authentic change with the unconditional love and fierceness of compassion is purely and utterly healing.

composting our pain into change

In 2009 I went on my first three-day meditation retreat. The retreat was titled "Healing the Heart," and it was specifically designed to guide participants through the messy and muddy waters of—you have probably guessed it—heartbreak. I had just gotten really serious about my daily meditation practice and living my life in alignment. Even back then, I unwittingly started to court my chitta—that is, my heart-minded consciousness—and flirt with living a heart-based life, one where my heart's wisdom was guiding me and showing me the way back to feeling whole again. I showed up to the retreat with a ton of woundedness and suffering from a dramatic and instant life change three years before. The process of healing had been slow and murky. I was just beginning to stand on my own two feet again, though every inch I walked on was still shaky with the tremors of change from life as I had once known it.

Intuitively I knew to begin the composting process of turning my suffering into wisdom, my brokenness into wholeness, and my imperfect shame into love. I had to do the inner work of looking my pain right in the eyes. The truth is, I hadn't mustered the courage to do so. I hadn't been strong enough to make that choice. We spent the first two days of the retreat creating the right container and conditions to look deeply into our heart's suffering. We were up at 4:00 a.m. and meditating by 5:00 a.m. Then, after breakfast, we went to work. Spending the rest of our days locating, naming, and writing our stories, the personal reasons of what brought us there. Each of us was asked to bravely identify and confront what had unraveled in our life, or what abrupt eruption had dismantled our reality. We were to name the loss, betrayal, divorce, separation, or unmet manifestation that had landed us in the truth of "I have some heart work to do."

My heart needed healing. I found this initial recognition process to be cathartic and relieving in itself. As I held my own heart with courage and clarity, I could see how I had not wanted to accept my pain and brokenness. I had done a lot of work to tuck it away, to hide it, making it as undetectable as I possibly could. We so often don't want to appear broken or bruised to others, especially those we don't know so well, such as a new team we are joining in the workplace. Or like on that first date, when musing about likes and interests, we wonder, "Will this person accept me and understand me for who I am? Could they, will they, love me for me and who I want to be?"

On the second evening of the retreat, we were asked to share our stories with the person sitting across from us in a circle: What was the cause of your heart needing healing? What was the unmentionable, shameful cause that brought you here? A cloud of murmurs and whispers began to emerge alongside sniffles and sounds of tears. Some of us, including me, had never before spoken out loud our deepest-kept secrets of suffering. I squirmed when the instructions of our group practice were shared. I wondered what would happen after I shared the painful secrets of my heart. Would I be rejected and judged for all of my brokenness?

Initially I kept my gaze downward at my hands as I met my discomfort, not wanting to look in the direction of the kind-eyed woman sitting across from me. Mentally I was probably scanning for an exit strategy, any way to avert exposure and vulnerability. Then my awareness started to pick up on the sounds of the room. The whispering of darkest moments of grief, depression, financial hardship, loss, and family problems came into focus. My ears detected some audible words: "inconceivable," "I can't forgive myself," "My weight is embarrassing," "I never told her I loved her." The more keenly I listened, the better I was able to perceive the palpable humming courage, bravery, and vulnerability of my fellow meditators in the room around me. The space had turned into a sound bath of seeing and holding each other's sufferings alongside our own. Shocked, I thought to myself, "This pain actually sounds . . . *beautiful* right now." I took a deep breath, looked up, and said to myself, "Well, let's just see how this goes."

Still with a knot of fear on the inside, I leaned over and whispered a wound into my partner's ear, right as the next group instruction sounded over the room's speaker: "Okay, after your partner shares what is asking for healing in their heart, it's the listener's turn to respond. And your response will be 'Thank you for telling me about your pain and heartbreak. And . . . I love you anyway.'" As these words were spoken in response, my insides softened and this seed of new understanding began to sink in: "I can be loved anyway, regardless of my past, my pain, and my brokenness."

We all left that retreat a little lighter. In just three days the group had become connected through one another's acceptance, understanding, and compassion. Seeing someone with love and tears of compassion and empathy in their eyes as they said to me, after receiving my deepest wound, "And . . . I love you anyway"—I felt personal healing at my core. The experience taught me how real healing and inner change happen when acceptance, nonjudgment, and the courage to be vulnerable are present—vulnerable with yourself first and foremost, and vulnerable with someone else when you are ready.

Fear of nonacceptance, rejection, and judgment is baked into our tender, cracked-open humanness. The need to present as perfect, as if we have our lives together, can stifle the creation of the right causes and conditions for real change to take hold in our lives. Fear can hijack our ability to keep choosing what we want and are working toward. And fear of judgment in particular can make us forget that compassion is possible. This can come through feeling paralyzed or stuck in negative patterns, or distrustful of exposing where we are at in the process of real change.

The brahma-viharas are the means to approaching real change as the practice of living your love and your inherent right to choose love again and again. Love is a choice, just like choosing to begin again with your meditation practice or to actualize your deepest intentions. The next step is to begin the twenty-eight days of heart practice, which will change you from the core and essence of your heart, from the inside out. I want you to keep in mind the following three principles that will keep you on track with letting real change take root in the loving spaciousness of compassion.

change as a compassion practice

1. SEEING WITH UNDERSTANDING. See your story, your past, and your pain as a friend and a teacher. As much as you can, practice seeing and being with any of your heart's

discomfort or healing just as you would with a dear friend and loved one during their growth and healing process. See your pain as an ally or a part of your history that doesn't define you but will lead you to greater strength and wisdom.

2. **LET YOUR PAIN SERVE A PURPOSE.** You may be reading this right now and thinking to yourself, "I'm so not there yet, Amanda." And to that I say, I get it. In fact, I more than get it. Here, I propose you try on letting your challenges be of service. Can anything you have gone through be of service to the healing of someone else in their journey? The author and holocaust survivor Viktor Frankl puts it this way: "In some way, suffering ceases to be suffering at the moment it finds a meaning."[4]

3. **CONNECT THROUGH KINDNESS.** The change you desire to see in yourself and in the world requires the brave vulnerability to connect with your suffering and hunger for healing and to offer this same sense of acceptance, understanding, and safe belonging to others. Kindness in this way becomes the vehicle in which you offer this safety and compassion to transmute and transform your past pain into the authentic intentional change you see for yourself and others.

Real change and healing begin when you are able to see yourself in others, and when you feel that your process of becoming who you are and want to be inspires and uplifts others' hearts. Choosing love and compassion each giant leap or stumbling step of the way allows for kindness to infuse you and exude from you, so much so it becomes the healing energy you leave in your wake.

———

I hope you are as excited as I am for the next twenty-eight days of discovering your truth, living your deepest intentions, and becoming the change you wish to be in the world. With the heart qualities of kindness, compassion, appreciative joy, and equanimity, you will be building an unshakable sense of home and belonging, love and strength, perseverance and self-worth. And you will do this each and every day you make the choice to practice becoming, transforming, and changing into who you already are and who you already know you can be. Trust that this is possible, that real change is possible, through aligning with the truth in your heart and by choosing to practice kindness now, as many times as you may need to.

TEACHINGS ON LOVING-KINDNESS

Metta is a vehicle to transform, open, and awaken your heart. Not only is it the first of the brahma-viharas but it also serves as the foundation of your heart practice you are beginning to develop today. The Pali word *metta* is often translated as "loving-kindness" or "friendliness." As a practice, it teaches us how to extend genuine kindness and friendship to ourselves and then outwardly to others. *Metta* is also translated as " love." I have found thinking of metta through these three facets— kindness, friendliness, and love—to be extremely helpful when adding metta into meditation practice. One of the main purposes of the heart practices is to be able to meet yourself and the situations, circumstances, and setbacks that you find yourself in through these three facets of metta. Meeting your moment-to-moment experience with metta alone will begin to change your relationship to the daily human moments we all encounter. Further, metta will also make you feel better in the magical medicinal kind of way it is known for.

kindness, friendliness, and love

On one day, you might find metta will be most useful in the form of total unfiltered kindness. The warm wash of real kindheartedness will be exactly what is needed when facing guilt about saying something you didn't mean to say or a lapse in judgment or a mistake. On another day, metta will be most useful in the form of friendship. The very concept of becoming your own inner bestie—offering yourself a hand of friendship, genuinely having your own back in the face of adversity, meeting yourself with kindness instead of judgment—changes the quality of your life. When you learn to give unwavering, caring, nonjudgmental friendship to your own heart and mind, soon you'll find natural friendliness more easily extendable to others, such as the people you work with, your good pals, or your difficult family members.

Then, on other days and in your most needed moments, metta will be most useful and medicinal in the form of love—that is, real love; not to be confused with romantic love or the type of love we normally think about or even aspire to in a personal way. In one of its strongest manifestations, metta is the conscious choice to respond with the presence of love, acceptance, and nonjudgmental compassion instead of the commonly hardwired reactionary fear or hatred. Love dissipates our past conditioning, painful cycles of unconscious reactionary patterns, and the obstacles faced when learning to love in a way we may never have loved before—the wise way.

The purpose of metta is to become heart-based and unbounded in our ability to truly love, to meet fear and difficulty with love, and to face our own anxious and fearful tendencies without the harshness of judgment. If you have ever felt like your mind is a kind of perilous place to be at times. Or if you have some pretty negative and nasty self-narratives circling on repeat (hello, inner critic). Such as, "I'm not pretty enough, thin enough, or fashionable enough to really put myself out there online or to date right now"; "I need to be more put together"; "I need to be more prepared for the meeting with my team lead that I've known about for over a week." Metta is going to prescriptively change the narrative by infusing it with kindness, friendliness, and love, one metta moment at a time.

aspirations versus affirmations

Metta is an aspirational practice that is different from repeating positive affirmations to ourselves. Aspiration practices are focused on willingness. Are you *willing* to wholeheartedly plant the seeds of well-being you want to embody and bloom in your heart? Are you *willing* to put in effort and intention when it's not so easy to be kind, forgiving, or compassionate with someone who has hurt you or not followed through on something they said they were going to do? Are you *willing* to stretch your heart and grow it beyond its current comfort zone and offer loving-kindness, appreciative joy, and empathy even when you don't want to?

Metta is training to love unconditionally, remaining open instead of closing down, and staying with yourself and your discomfort even when it's not your first choice to do so. It is also the aspiration to not abandon yourself or others along the path of being human and gaining wisdom from your heartbreak and mistakes. Your greatest aspirations will take the biggest willingness from deep within you. Aspirations allow for the willingness to not abandon any piece or part of your life, which takes a resilience that can only be found in the heart.

Affirmations, which reside in the mental plane only, are statements or phrases telling you to be, do, or feel a certain way even when you may not feel that way in the moment. Affirmations are good reminders of what you aspire to, yet reminders will not get you very far without the strength required from the heart. Aspirations give you room and permission to grow into the qualities that you wish for and intend for, often with the much-needed support of patience, kindness, and allowance for imperfection. The more you practice metta, the more you will find out exactly where in your life your heart is open, where it's still shut down, and where there's room for growth.

One way I like to think of practicing metta is by viewing each phrase as a seed holding an intention that I would like to plant for myself or others. When I say to myself, "May I be happy," "May Anna be happy," or "May Mark be happy," each repetition represents planting a seed of the intention embedded within a wish. I am planting a seed for happiness deep within the layers of my heart and mind.

Metta is much like gardening: when the season, causes, and conditions are right; and with the right care, sunlight, and nutrients; whatever specific intentions and aspirational qualities you plant eventually will begin to root and flower.

how to practice

- Silently repeat metta mantras (phrases)—genuine wishes for kindness, friendliness, and love that emanate from the heart and mind.
- Rest your attention on the metta phrases and the feelings that emanate from these very intentional wishes.

METTA TOWARD SELF

The motivation to implement any great change or shift in our lives has to come from within. The same is true with metta. Therefore, Days 1 through 4 in *Kindness Now* are focused on sending metta toward yourself. In doing so, you are training to meet yourself with kindness, love, acceptance, forgiveness, nonjudgment, and any heart quality that is needed at any given moment.

METTA TOWARD OTHERS

On Day 5, you'll learn to send metta outward to others: to people you know well and who you hold dear, as well as to those you don't know personally at all, such as a cashier at your market-place or a neighbor you only see walking down the street. But you do so not at the expense of your own well-being. For so many of my students, this is a powerful insight: the understanding that you can wish someone happiness and ease without detracting from your own equilibrium or well-earned joy.

METTA TOWARD DIFFICULT PEOPLE

Day 6 is particularly relevant to a category of "others" known traditionally as "difficult people." At first thought of these difficult people, you might say to yourself, "There is no way I can send *them* loving-kindness. Not after what they did, said, didn't say, or how much they hurt me." This is exactly why you include them in your metta practice—so that you can understand where you are feeling limited or conditional with your heart's wishes and train yourself to still open your heart even when it's not easy to do so.

METTA TOWARD THE WORLD

Naturally, when you practice metta, it will point you to the innate interconnectedness we all share with every single being in the world. That's right—even nonhuman beings, so metta toward all beings is Day 7's practice. One of my favorite stories I hear from my students practicing metta is when they find them-selves sending loving-kindness to their dog or a feathery friend such as a bird chirping outside their window. Since real love is boundless, we choose to include all living beings everywhere, near and far, when we send metta out to the world at large.

PRACTICE NOTE: As you are just beginning your metta practice, remember this is when you will need the heart qualities the most. Just as it takes time to train your mind and attention to be in the present moment, training the heart's capacity for loving-kindness, compassion, appreciative joy, and equanimity takes time and patience as well.

The Buddhist teacher Chögyam Trungpa Rinpoche says, just as "everybody is capable of falling in love; everybody is capable of being kind to others."[5] Just as we have all fallen in love before, we all have the same default ability to be kind. To be human is also to know inextricably how to care for ourselves and others. It's just part of the deal and part of our primordial DNA. Since kindness is a muscle too, this week will guide you in growing and strengthening the kindness muscle you already have within you. Metta is the vehicle and tool we use to bring us back home to who we already are and it all begins with ground zero—you.

DAY 1

---

ground zero: you

I have heard it all my life,
A voice calling a name I recognized as my own.
—Oriah Mountain Dreamer

WELCOME TO THE first day of the rest of your life! That's right, you have decided to take an extraordinary next step, not only in your meditation practice but also in transforming and changing how you meet yourself and your daily life. Just like with any contemplative and spiritual practice, we first must do the work within in order to see the tangible changes on the outside, so we start close to home with metta. Step 1, or ground zero, is you.

Today's practice lays the important groundwork of learning how to wish yourself loving-kindness and remove common obstacles to receiving the healing effects of metta. One of the first blocks I see when beginning a metta practice is the well-known and often deeply entrenched feeling of unworthiness. Somewhere deep down we feel as though we don't deserve our own kindness or the healing that comes with real inner friendliness and unbounded self-love. Countless times I have heard meditation students reflect just how much easier it is to wish happiness, health, and well-being to someone else than it is to wish it to themselves. It is one of the most frequent reflections I hear from people just starting to explore any of the brahma-viharas. So many of us grapple with the concept of self-worth, never mind the worthiness of receiving genuine goodness and well-being. Chronic undeservingness and unworthiness is a modern emotional epidemic. It is one of the biggest hurdles to overcome.

let's check in

When first beginning your metta practice, it is wise to check in with your fundamental level of worthiness. Being able to receive your own wishes for happiness, health, abundance, safety, peace, and well-being is a form of self-worth.

Pause and notice what comes up when you read this. If you sense that presently you have a low level of self-worth, stop and move into this first exercise right now.

Write down your top ten strengths and lovable traits. Think *respect and admiration* while you are writing these down.

REFLECTION QUESTION 1: What do others love and respect about you? What type of help do they turn to you for?

REFLECTION QUESTION 2: More importantly, what do *you* love and value or appreciate about yourself? Is it how you are always there for others? Or how strong you are and how much you have overcome? Is it your natural generosity? Or your healthy obsession with following through and keeping your word? Now go ahead and write these traits down in your practice journal. And after you've completed this first writing check-in, make sure to note that you can reflect back on this list of lovable traits anytime you start to feel unworthy.

Just as mindfulness purifies the mind of its preconditioning, metta purifies our hearts of the preexisting relationships we have with ourselves. These underlying relationships are often based on the past and not even necessarily still true in the present moment. Until you start an intentional practice of expanding your heart's ability to be kind, noncritical, and free from fear, the overall feeling you hold toward yourself will largely remain unconscious. Metta reminds us of our birthright to feel good, feel worthy, feel whole, and let ourselves off the hook for our past mistakes.

Metta invites us to accept a basic level of self-gifted kindness and to feel worthy of receiving exactly what it is we truly know we need, want, and desire deep down in our hearts. In metta practice, we train toward this fundamental deservingness—a profound sense of feeling worthy enough to accept the natural generosity of our hearts purely because we are alive. Sensing and receiving metta toward ourselves says "I value you, I love you, and I believe in your deservingness. Just like any other being that is alive, I too deserve to feel happy, peaceful, and free."

Taking this first step to being able to wish yourself metta and receive your own kindness is going to lay the groundwork for the rest of our month together. And don't worry if it feels a bit awkward at first. Remember, metta, just like mindfulness, is a practice. It will take time, dedication, and patience to train and expand your heart muscle.

Go ahead and get settled into your meditation space. Have your practice journal and a pen or pencil next to you.

today's meditation

LOVING-KINDNESS TOWARD SELF

- Allow your body to find a comfortable posture.
- Take three deep breaths.

- Center yourself in your body by softening any areas of tension.
- Place your attention on the natural breath.
- Follow the breath for a few breath cycles.
- Allow your focus to move to the area of your heart.
- Sense your heartbeat or try placing your hands over your heart.
- With a sense of connection to your heart, silently wish yourself the following metta mantras.

metta mantras

May I be happy.
May I be healthy.
May I release anything blocking me from well-being.
May I allow metta to meet me today or someday soon.

- Repeat today's metta mantras three times.
- Rest your attention back in your heart.
- Take a deep breath in and exhale.
- Gently open your eyes when you are ready.

Now get ready for today's contemplation practice. You may want to jot a few meditation insights down in your practice journal before moving into today's reflection question. Think of these reflection questions as a second practice after meditation. These mindful inquiries will help guide you into the deeper layers of your mind and heart.

PRACTICE NOTE: Metta phrases have been used in Buddhist meditation for thousands of years. While traditional metta phrases are broadly practiced and proven to be quite useful, making metta personal also makes it the most meaningful.

You want to feel comfortable with and connected to the wishes and aspirations you are planting for yourself and your life.

So today's first reflection question will help you get clear on what it is you truly want to wish for yourself in your heart. Think of this wish as your deepest intention and dearest desire. Making metta your own through contemplating what your heart's wisdom wants for you and placing this deep intention into a wish through your own personal metta phrase will be not only a heart opener for you to let metta start to flow in. It is also a way to really kick open the doors for metta to start to take hold in your heart and mind.

Have your practice journal and pen ready. Close your eyes for a moment and take a deep breath in and out as you connect back to your heart space. Then when you are ready, ask yourself today's reflection question.

REFLECTION QUESTION: What do I wish and want for myself? What is my deepest wish?

Allow any answers to arise. Pause long enough to listen and receive your own heart's advice and wisdom. Silently thank your heart and take a deep breath and open your eyes. Start journaling your insights and answers. Write down your main wishes for yourself in the following metta-phrase structure:

May I _____ (fill in with the heart-based quality that is most meaningful to you. For example, "May I know peace. May I let go of the need to control. May I feel better. May I release fear. May I welcome the new. May I learn to love without limits.")

After you've written down your mantra, close your eyes once again and repeat your personal metta mantra to yourself silently in your mind three times. Inhale deeply, then exhale, and slowly open your eyes. You now have your own personal metta mantra to bring with you as you meditate and move into the rest of your day!

PRACTICE NOTE: Metta can be practiced not only while you are in meditation but also in the moment and on the fly. Think of this as an extra-fun way to deepen your practice and let metta get in and support you in all of life's areas.

TODAY'S METTA MOMENT

Your first daily metta moment is to pause at least three times and send yourself your personal metta mantra. Set a reminder in your schedule today for midmorning, lunch, in the afternoon, or before dinner to gently and silently repeat your metta mantra in your mind and with your attention centered in your heart. Trust me, this will so metta-fy your day. It will keep you connected to your heart's awareness, focused on what you truly wish and desire for yourself. It will also help you in building the life-changing habit of wishing yourself genuine well-being and kindness.

————

DAY 2

---

becoming your own bff

I got my own back.
—*Maya Angelou*

IT IS POSSIBLE to become your own best friend, I promise. One of the many things meditation teaches us is that there is a sweet, subtle healing available when we become comfortable spending time in our own company. *Metta*, as you have learned, means "friendship." You are cultivating a feeling of loving friendliness, and what better person to start with than yourself. Though, as you may have discovered on Day 1, this isn't always the easiest practice. Why? Becoming your own BFF requires real inner work. As you'll continue to discover in your unique way this month, the heart practices aren't necessarily for the faint of heart.

my road to self-friendship

For fifteen years I was a serial monogamist. I moved from one relationship right into another, often without even being single for more than a week. On one hand, I felt very lucky to have one wonderful man after another step into my life. Each of my partners was a truly exceptional person in his own right, and some were among my greatest teachers. Yet five relationships in, and a number of years into my meditation practice, two truths began to become undeniably clear: (1) I didn't really know what it was like to be in my own company. I was rarely physically alone and never really inwardly alone. It seemed I was constantly giving, caring for, and tending to my partner's needs, preferences, and desires, often over my own. (2) I was dependent on my boyfriends to feel whole and complete as a person. Unknowingly over the years, I had given my sense of self over to my partners, while simultaneously abandoning my own sense of center and authentic home within. I had become highly codependent. I was constantly fearful of not being able to support myself emotionally and financially, and I was nowhere near the vibrational feeling of having my own back or being my own unconditional best friend.

As modern, busy people, many of us are not used to facing our inner world and finding the courage to rest in our unique stillness and solitude. In fact, one of the most common reasons people abandon meditation practice, even after starting with all the right intentions, is because they become more aware of who they are, including their inadequacies, imperfections, and flaws. Without approaching our inner landscape with a flag of friendship in hand, readily waving it, many of us get freaked out and completely abandon the inner work all together. We are unfamiliar with slowing down and meeting our inner world with a sense of curiosity, respect, and unconditional kindness.

The breakup that ended the five-relationship-straight streak of never being on my own was largely spawned from my growing inner awareness of such tendencies. The day I ended the last relationship was after a daylong meditation retreat with one of my mentors that happened to be on the topics of awareness and love. We didn't talk about love in the traditional sense of romanticism or between two people. We practiced metta—being friendly toward what we became aware of when resting in our own inner stillness. It was during this day of inner solitude when I finally became strong enough *and* soft enough to listen to the voice calling from deep within my heart—a voice I had shut out, suppressed, and denied over the years. When I finally became willing and genuinely kind and still enough, it offered me the hand of inner friendship, saying with total confidence and clarity, "Amanda, it is time to let go of this painful love. It is time to be on your own. It's time to get back to your center."

Metta holds this capacity to befriend ourselves in a deep, intimate, and honest way. Real self-love—loving, unconditional friendliness—is born from metta. It's through the extended hand of inner friendship that we learn to not reject ourselves and to accept all parts of ourselves. Through unconditional friendliness we learn to not abandon ourselves—no matter how many mistakes we've made or how much we've messed up—and to finally, courageously listen to what our heart has to say. The meditation teacher Sharon Salzberg, author of *Lovingkindness* puts it like this: "The foundation of metta practice is to know how to be our own friend."[6]

befriending your mind

To say yes to becoming your own BFF is one of the greatest moments of healing and gifts you can ever give to yourself. And just as with mindfulness, where you choose to return to the present moment and begin again an unfathomable number of times during the course of your lifetime, with metta you can choose to offer yourself friendship over and over again as many times as you need to. Meditation is the training ground to practice this unconditional friendship with yourself, especially when it comes to navigating one of the biggest perceived obstacles to finding calm and peace in meditation, which is . . . drum roll . . . the thoughts in your mind.

To start Day 2, let's cultivate this inner capacity to meet ourselves with genuine friendliness instead of judgment or aversion. We'll focus particularly on the mental layer of thinking, where it is often so easy to avoid, repress, abandon, and negate ourselves.

Go ahead and get settled into your meditation space. Just like yesterday, have your practice journal and a pen or pencil next to you. Take a deep breath, and let's begin.

---

today's meditation

SMILING AT YOUR THOUGHTS

- Let your attention start to settle into your body as you find a comfortable posture.
- Invite three deep breaths, inhaling and exhaling gently.
- Scan your body from head to toe with a tone of friendliness and kindness.
- Now, guide your attention back to the sensations of the breath.
- Each time you become aware of a thought crossing through your mind, meet this thought with a loving smile. You can visualize an internal smile each time you notice a thought, or you can physically smile, softly turning the corners of your lips upward (just like a happy smiling buddha).
- Continue this practice of internally or physically smiling at your thoughts and then guiding your attention back to the sensations of the breath.
- Then add the metta mantra as you smile at your thoughts.

metta mantra

May I meet my thoughts with a smile.

- Silently repeat this metta mantra for the duration of your meditation practice.
- To end, take a deep breath and slowly open your eyes.

Learning to meet your thoughts with a smile plants seeds for meeting your full self with unconditional loving awareness. Since you are setting your metta foundation this week, move into the following reflection that will guide you in noticing what is preventing you from befriending yourself. Get ready to release any weeds of self-aversion with the following contemplation.

Have your practice journal and pen ready. If you'd like you can close your eyes for a moment. Take a deep breath in and out. Connect to your heart space and ask yourself today's reflection question.

REFLECTION QUESTION: What are my main obstacles to being my own BFF?

Repeat this question as many times as you need to. When you start to notice answers arise, settle your attention on them for a moment. Meet them with a tone of friendliness, just as you would with a dear friend. Thank the answers for showing themselves to you. Take a breath and open your eyes.

Write down your obstacles to self-love or friendship in your practice journal. Let the words flow. Once you have written down your obstacles, close your eyes and take a moment to thank your heart for the courage required to show you where you are blocked. Promise to meet these obstacles with compassion and understanding. Inhale and exhale once more, and when you are ready, open your eyes.

TODAY'S METTA MOMENT

Continue to meet your thoughts today with an inner smile and practice becoming your own BFF by not judging or abandoning yourself when any of your obstacles come up. Metta is a muscle and a practice of growing your foundation of self-safety and support. It will take patience and practice, so be psyched to begin this practice of learning to befriend yourself and your thoughts starting today. And remember, you can begin again as many times as you need to.

———

DAY 3

---

may i meet this too with kindness

Practice kindness all day to everybody and
you will realize you're already in heaven now.
—Jack Kerouac

THE WAY WE START to transform our daily lives all comes down to *how* we meet our lives. This *how* shows us the magic of kindness and the limitless love of the heart. Metta moves us from harshness to kindness and from judgment back to joy. This radical shift can be rather subtle at first. For instance, you may be used to letting the pesky and often rampant inner critic have free rein over your mind all day and feel guilt over all your relentless negative self-talk. However, after you've made the commitment to practice kindness now, what once led to shame and that pit of tightness in your chest now is met, in the face of your metta-filled heart and mind, with a kinder, warmer nod of acknowledgment as you become aware of your self-talk's tone. You may even be able to muster a wise, compassionate wave to your recurring afflictive emotions. Kindness has the power to intervene with all of the unwanted guests in our human guesthouse: "Ah, anxiety, fear, meanness, self-deprecation—here you are again, my dear old friends."

welcome in radical inclusion

If you have been meditating for some time, most likely you have gotten to know yourself a little more. Even as you've been meditating over these past two days using this book, you may have noticed your thoughts and the surprising imprints of these thoughts: the residue those nagging emails from your boss leave in your mind, the restlessness stemming from the laundry list of items you need to get for your house or apartment, the anxiety over the number in your bank account, or the overall discontent from all the things that maybe aren't going exactly how you want them to.

As meditators, we inevitably discover that awareness isn't necessarily the problem. We have become well aware of the rotating guests of emotions and the well-worn grooves of negative habitual thinking in our minds all day long. What's left in our hands and upon our hearts is what to do with what we become aware of. How do we meet all that is rummaging through our inner landscape?

Metta practice is how you will really start to see the transformational medicine of kindness. It's how we make peace with these undesired guests, an internal truce that lets the incredible alchemy of the heart unfold in our daily lives.

This kind, well-meaning approach toward our hearts and minds helps us move in the life directions we want to be going in while being more accepting and compassionate about our setbacks, failures, and habits of self-sabotage. The moment I began to welcome my unwanted guests with kindness—sending metta toward each thought, feeling, and corner of sadness in my heart—is when I felt the first taste of real healing in my life.

Meeting what is present with kindness teaches us the profound lesson of letting go into our human experience, even into all of the unwanted stuff. Ultimately it gives us the resources of compassion, bigheartedness, and inclusivity, so much so that I've come to call self-kindness a practice of radical inclusion. Only real kindness lets us do that. It keeps us from turning away from our unwanted thoughts, memories, idiosyncrasies, and experiences and gives them the respect and room to be here. This simple spaciousness is the doorway into the heart.

Today brings you to one of the most important bridge crossings in your meditation practice: the bridge from what to how—from self-awareness to self-kindness and inclusion with the powerhouse metta mantra introduced to me by one of my mindfulness mentors, Diana Winston.

That's right, I will guide you in learning how to meet anything that you become aware of in meditation or daily life with kindness. You will most likely feel the immediate relief that the medicine of loving-kindness brings to your inner world.

Now, let's get to work and have you start meeting all that is here with kindness now.

today's meditation

A SELF-KINDNESS MEDITATION

- Go ahead and get settled in for your time in meditation today.
- Let the body find its most comfortable posture, with your spine tall and your chest and ribcage feeling open.
- Gently close your eyes and breathe in and out with a deep understanding that you are here, in your body, in this present moment.

- Allow your breath to become your reminder to keep your attention in the present.
- Each time your attention wanders to any thoughts in your mind or any feelings or sensations in your body, repeat the following metta mantra.

metta mantra

May I meet this too with kindness.

- Repeat this phrase of loving-kindness toward your thoughts, feelings, or sensations as many times as you need to.
- Then guide your attention back to the anchor of the breath once again.
- Go ahead and practice in this way for the duration of your meditation.
- To end, take a deep breath in and out, and when you are ready, open your eyes.

Now, move right into today's contemplation. Get your practice journal and pen. Connect back to your loving heart space. Close your eyes for a moment. Take a deep breath in and out and ask yourself today's reflection question and pick up your practice journal and pen.

REFLECTION QUESTION: How does it feel when I meet myself with kindness instead of judgment or reaction?

Let any answers flow onto the page. When you are finished, silently thank your heart and practice. Take a deep breath and bring these metta gifts into the rest of your day!

TODAY'S METTA MOMENT

Learning to meet yourself with kindness is the gift of metta meditation. It is the medicine your heart and inner life yearns for as you are so used to meeting yourself with all kinds of judgment and past conditioning.

Today, as you move through the day, I want you to repeat today's metta mantra silently in your mind whenever you notice you are being hard on yourself, judgmental toward yourself, or unkind in any way. Extend this practice toward anything that occurs in your day or to anyone. Focus particularly in the realm of unpleasant moments or feelings, or when things aren't going the way you would like them to. Lean into your new metta mantra and train to meet all that is here with kindness.

DAY 4

---

from self-hate to self-love

*Self-respect is a discipline, a habit of
mind that can never be faked but can be
developed, trained, coaxed forth.*
—Joan Didion

DAY 4 IS A BIG DAY. So to start, place your hand on your heart and take a long deep breath right from the center of your being. As you take this deep breath, rest your attention in your heart space for a moment. Notice what feeling tone or mood is there presently, and just as you learned yesterday, see if you can conjure kindness as you become aware of what's here in your heart today.

Kindness is both the seed and the delicate little roots that sprout turning your intentions for self-love into a strong, growing seedling of reality. When we develop loving-kindness, or *maitri* in Sanskrit, we are "placing our fearful mind in the cradle of loving-kindness."[7] In many ways, to genuinely feel love toward ourselves and to understand our own loving nature, we must also see our fear, delusion, avoidance, and hatred in a clear and honest way. To have self-love we must first see what is blocking our ability to extend natural warmth and love toward ourselves.

So let's explore some very common blocks many of us have to feeling connected to our innate loving nature and wellspring of self-love for a moment, beginning with self-hatred.

uncovering your self-respect

Self-hatred can have many facets to it. It's like the invisible elephant in the room, taking up all of the available space, stomping and trumpeting about, while we often are left wondering why we feel so uneasy. For some, self-hatred is easy to identify. It's most present as an underlying sentiment of self-directed loathing, a feeling of constant discontent, a debilitating state of fearful thinking, the inner critical voice that is relentless, or the feeling of being behind or not good enough unless every item on the to-do list is achieved.

For others, self-hatred is subtler. It is the wounding and suffering we silently live with and may be largely unaware of. It's the tightness in our chest; the self-deprecating beliefs we adopted from our parents or caregivers; the self-aggression of being anything but automatically kind, understanding, or forgiving toward ourselves. When we are caught in the wheelhouse of self-hatred, we have yet to earn our own gift of self-respect. Self-respect means in a fundamental way that we kinda like ourselves. We have a healthy view of who we are as a person and feel good about ourselves even when we make mistakes or tend toward unconsciously self-sabotaging actions. As Chögyam Trungpa Rinpoche describes, "Maitri is based on being gentle with yourself, and at the same time respecting yourself."[8] Self-respect stems from a softened way of relating to our inner world. Through gentleness we can extend the generosity of empathy, compassion, and friendliness to ourselves. Over time, this way of self-relating becomes the new baseline. Our default response will be choosing to meet ourselves and others with kindness, to let go of any confusion around separateness, and to learn to place the fearful mind, any judgments, and self-deprecation into the cradle of loving-kindness.

melting the inner ice

Self-hatred has historically been one of my main roots of personal suffering. I wasn't even aware of how much my unconscious lack of love toward myself was running the show until I went on my first metta meditation retreat, where I learned the different stages of loving-kindness.

It was still toward the beginning of the week, much like we are now in your twenty-eight days of heart practice, where well into a period of metta meditation directed toward the self I began to become aware of my self-hatred for the very first time. At first I felt this block to my metta as a heavy closedness in my heart. Then a mental image arose of a tall dark mountain glacier, with sheets of gray glistening ice covering its sides. Its cold presence made my heart feel smaller and smaller; my body slumped over trying to protect me from the painful constricting cold. As I held this meeting of my self-hatred for the first time, I remembered the instructions I had received from our retreat leaders earlier that day: "Can you give yourself the respect and reverence of turning toward your difficulties, pain, and fear, just enough so you are really free to feel what arises?" So I gave myself the respect of feeling my self-hatred; even as my spine shuttered and fear coursed through me, I continued to send metta toward the icy gray glacier I had just uncovered in my heart. And after meeting it with a kind-intentioned respect like the gentle heat of the winter sun, my glacier of self-hatred started to melt and turn into a beautiful roaring waterfall nourishing a green meadow that had formed just below it. I realized right in the middle of my meditation practice that this life-giving waterfall was self-love made directly from my thawed glacier of self-hatred.

This morning, many years later, I woke up to the very first conscious thoughts moving through my mind: "I love you, be kind to yourself today." My heart instantly softened and felt nourished by this innate loving-kindness toward myself right upon waking. Tears are welling up in my eyes as I write these words to you now, because it hasn't always been this way. In fact, since that day I met my glacier of self-hatred for the very first time, I've had to remind myself countless times to meet myself with that same warming kindness that melted my self-hatred into the waters of self-love.

Today I'm going to share this very same meditation with you from my first metta retreat. It has been both a constant reminder to choose love over self-flagellation and to make the inner promise to be kind daily. In today's meditation you will visualize your inner capacity for warmth and self-love as a beautiful radiating sun melting away any remnants of fear or self-dislike. Follow my guidance and get ready to melt your blocks to self-love.

today's meditation

RADIATING SUN OF KINDNESS VISUALIZATION

- Go ahead and get comfortable. Position the palms of your hands facing upward, to cultivate an open, loving state.
- Close your eyes and take a deep breath in and out.
- Now, lightly rest your attention in your body and imagine a bright, beautiful radiating sunrise. As this sun starts to brighten in the sky, the night's darkness fades away.
- Feel the warmth from the sun's rays resting on your forehead, cheeks, and the sides of your face.

- Any tension your body is holding effortlessly melts away.
- Your body fully relaxes and your mind starts to feel at ease.
- As you rest in this radiating sun of self-kindness and love, you notice that any feelings of ill will, self-hatred, or self-criticism are met with an unconditional gentleness from your inner sunshine.
- Resentment or fear starts to dissolve, just like a glacier of icy snow turning to water and then nourishing the green meadows below.
- The warmth from your sun of kindness fills your body, mind, and heart with the unwavering tenderness of self-love.
- Continue to rest in this state of self-love for the remaining minutes of your meditation.
- When your meditation time is complete, slowly open your eyes.

Now, it's time for today's contemplation. Get your practice journal and pen ready. Take a deep breath and ask yourself today's reflection questions.

REFLECTION QUESTION 1: What can I let go of and allow to melt away?

REFLECTION QUESTION 2: In what ways can I invite in self-love?

Let all of your thoughts, answers, and insights pour onto the page. When your pen comes to a stop, take a deep breath, reconnect with your inner sun of loving-kindness, and meet the next present moments of your day.

TODAY'S METTA MOMENT

Self-love is a practice, and it may take some time to unwind all the years of relating to yourself in a different way. This is okay!

The sun still comes up every day regardless of what happened the day before. This is a real opportunity to stay connected to your natural capacity for maitri by viewing self-love as a quality to keep tending and opening to. At any time during your day today, you can reimagine your beautiful, bright radiating sun of self-kindness and self-love.

If you're feeling extra-metta-inspired, you can take cultivating maitri a step further today with this on-the-spot practice: anytime those old familiar feelings, thoughts, or tendencies of self-hatred stomp in thinking they will get their way, you can turn toward them with the confidence of the sun and say to yourself, "And . . . I love you anyway."

DAY 5

moving beyond just me

The highest form of love is the love that allows for
intimacy without the annihilation of difference.
—*Parker J. Palmer*

TO PRACTICE METTA is to train our ability to truly love. We're not talking about the usual kind of love, where someone wins our affection and we keep loving them contingent upon whether they do what we like or not. Metta moves us beyond our singular, personalized, often siloed experience of love and asks us to love in a much different way—a way that is more aligned with our true nature and the real nature of the heart. Metta asks us to train to be limitless and unrelenting with our love, unbounded and boundaryless. This type of love inspires us to step past our comfort zones of how we currently extend kindness, friendliness, and good-heartedness in our daily interactions and requires us to dig deeper and consider our way of relating with the world.

In many ways, metta is our greatest teacher of how to love another person or being. To move from dependent love—a love based on our personal likes, dislikes, and preferences—to independent love—a love that is free and unhinged from dependence on our personal or biased interests is how we meet our most genuine freedom. Real love is synonymous with real freedom; therefore we become free when we learn to offer our loving-kindness freely.

Just as with mindfulness, metta can be very helpful when it bridges our past and personal microcosms of existence to our relationships and daily lives. The past four days of practice have prepared you for this next step in the very strategic path of metta: moving your metta practice beyond just you to applying these same principles of loving-kindness, befriending, and basic respect outward. Just like when you send metta toward yourself, it's okay if you don't necessarily feel in that moment the exact sentiments that you are wishing for when you send it to others. Remember, metta is an aspirational practice. We aspire toward the wholesome qualities of the heart we know deep down will be of benefit.

our practice edges

When you begin practicing metta for others, one of the most insightful aspects of metta meditation will most likely arise: the awareness of where your heart is currently open or closed. I like to refer to this as "our practice edges." Almost immediately when sending metta toward others we quickly bump into where we feel limitless, free, open, and available with our love and where we feel constricted, hardened, or shut down. Metta is so intimate in this way. Like it or not, we realize where we are blocked in authentically wishing happiness and well-being to others. Whether it be to our childhood nemesis, the person talking loudly on their phone in front of us as we wait in line for coffee, or even someone who has broken our heart, betrayed our trust, or wronged us in some way, metta requires us to stretch our hearts in uncomfortable yet illuminating ways.

This little (or big) moment of self-awareness directly shows us where our natural capacity to limitlessly love begins and ends. The hardening of our hearts is also an opportunity to self-check and practice nonjudgment: "Ah, this is where my heart closes down. This is where I feel constricted and small again." It may be over the trivial inconvenience of someone cutting in front of us in the brunch line, or with that person who never lets us get a word in, or at that dog who just wouldn't stop barking all morning long.

Metta shows us our shadows while giving us opportunities to radically not judge our often suppressed or secret inner thoughts and feelings. I've taken on the attitude of reverently rejoicing when bumping into my practice edges or noticing my heart close down to offering metta toward another out of self-defense or fear. The moment I become aware that my genuine good wishing has shut down is the same moment I know there is healing available and whatever wound or perceived slight has just become workable.

To wish other beings genuine happiness, health, abundance, and well-being requires softening into our own fundamental goodness and aspirations. In today's practice you are going to move your metta from just you to what is traditionally known as a benefactor, and then to a neutral person. The benefactor is someone or something you already have a natural warmth toward. Your benefactor can be a beloved, a family member, or a good friend. The neutral person is someone who you feel simply neutral about—for whom you don't have strong feelings of unpleasantness or pleasantness; your heart or energy isn't pulled one way or the other.

Now let's put these principles into practice in today's meditation! You will widen your circle of metta beyond yourself and experience the insight and joy that comes from sending metta toward others.

LOVING-KINDNESS MEDITATION
TOWARD OTHERS

- Allow your body to find its way to a comfortable posture.
- Invite in three deep breaths, sensing your body receive fresh air on the inhale and noticing your body let go of the breath on the exhale. Close your eyes.
- Settle your attention in your body for the next few moments.
- Allow your awareness to rest in your heart as you breathe in and breathe out. With your presence anchored in your heart space, start to send metta toward yourself. Come into contact with the felt sense of loving-kindness, friendliness, and inner nonjudgment you've come to know over the past four days.
- Then begin to call to mind a beloved benefactor—someone or some being you strongly like or even love—to send metta to.
- See their image in your mind, feel their presence in your heart, silently say their name three times, or simply know who is receiving your metta.
- With this beloved benefactor in mind and heart, send them the same metta mantras you've been wishing toward yourself, or use the following phrases.

metta mantras

May you be happy.
May you be healthy.
May you be safe and protected.
May you live with ease.

- After sending these metta mantras, now let go of the image of your beloved benefactor.
- Lightly guide your attention back to the breath and your heart space.
- Call to mind a neutral person to whom you'd like to send your good wishes. This is someone you know but not so personally that you've formed a strong dislike or like toward them.
- Reflect that they want to be happy, healthy, and fulfilled just like you.
- Start to wish them the same phrases of metta that you were sending toward yourself and your beloved benefactor.
- When it's time to end, let the image of your neutral person dissolve from your mind.
- End by taking a long deep breath in and out, then slowly open your eyes.

Now, for the next few moments, take up your pen and practice journal and settle into the following contemplation.

REFLECTION QUESTION 1: Where was my heart open or closed when sending loving-kindness to others?

REFLECTION QUESTION 2: What did I notice when I sent metta toward others versus sending metta toward myself?

When you're done journaling, close your eyes, take a long deep breath, and thank your practice edges *and* your open-heartedness today.

PRACTICE NOTE: Some meditators find that it is actually easier to send metta toward others than to themselves. There isn't any particular way this practice should be or feel for you, so if that was the case, awesome. Or if you found it was a bit awkward to send metta toward others, or you felt disconnected from the phrases, equally okay. Remember, you are planting seeds of goodwill and friendliness when you practice metta. Overall, you are looking for the doorway into your heart of unconditional love. As you will come to find, there are many different doorways into this boundless heart.

TODAY'S METTA MOMENT

As you've learned, metta is also a very mobile practice. Really, it's a mindset and heart space you can cultivate even in your time off the cushion. One of my absolute favorite metta practices is "on-the-fly metta" or "spontaneous metta." This is the practice of sending metta toward others *spontaneously* in the moment at any time throughout your day. You may be walking down the street passing hundreds of people, if you live in an urban home such as New York City or London. Or if you live in a more rural setting, maybe you see several people in cars as you are driving toward town. Whether you see one person or countless people around you, send them the metta mantras of happiness and well-being as you pass them by. With a genuine feeling in your heart, silently say, "May you be happy and peaceful! May *your* day unfold with ease!" Keep wishing anyone and any being well. In fact, yesterday I sent loving-kindness to a woolly bear caterpillar I saw on the path as I was moving my body and enjoying my daily walk.

DAY 6

---

your difficult people

No Mud, No Lotus.
—*Thich Nhat Hanh*

THERE IS A COMMON SAYING in the meditation world that I return to over and over again: "No mud, no lotus." The peacemaker, humanitarian, and Buddhist monk Thich Nhat Hanh shares this phrase throughout his teachings on mindfulness, loving awareness, and how to meet our suffering.

As we learned on Day 5, metta will stretch us. Discovering our heart's capacity moves us into unresolved territories of the heart. It requires us to confront our personal practice edges. It asks us to grow and expand in ways that we may cognitively know are possible but that we haven't put into practice yet. This is the transformation zone, and it will be muddy. Especially when we start the practice of extending loving-kindness to the category of difficult ones.

our enemies are our greatest teachers

Traditionally, our difficult people are "our enemies." They trigger suffering within us. They close us down, frustrate us,

65

anger us, cause us to spin out or lose our cool. They may have harmed us outrightly in some way. These people may have been our perceived enemies for the past two decades, or they may have gained the more recent status of a "frenemy." Yet when it comes to loving-kindness practice, our enemies become a way for us to gauge our ability to extend unconditional love from our hearts. In truth, our enemies are our greatest teachers because they shovel the mud right onto our front doorsteps and give us the work of cleaning up the hurt, grievance, despair, or shame caused by their actions or words. This is why we include them in our circle of loving-kindness. We may be knee-deep in the mud of our suffering and hurt, but we are also resting in the fertile ground where our greatest lotuses can eventually bloom.

I've always had a hard time with conflict. Growing up, I was majorly conflict avoidant. When I had to have a difficult conversation or confront someone with whom I disagreed, the discord and negativity were way too much and sometimes would flatline me in bed for a whole afternoon or even days. My need to have everything "in harmony" always made the weight of difficulty a major obstacle to my happiness. If I was irritated, angered, or wronged by someone, I would avoid any confrontation with them yet harbor major resentment internally. These seeds of hurt, perceived injustice, or disrespect would grow inside of me and cause me to greatly suffer. I carried a lot of low-grade resentment toward others inside of me for many years.

When I first encountered the category of difficult people in metta practice, these same avoidant feelings came up. To look our hurt, hatred, and grievances square in the eye is far from fun, and it requires a lot of inner work and willingness to be in the thick of our inner mud. I remember being on a weeklong silent metta meditation retreat, approaching the practice of sending loving-kindness to our difficult people, when I recollected what I had learned in mindfulness. I sat there on the cushion saying to myself, "Well, all of these years of meditation have been training you to stay here in this present moment. If anything, you've discovered sometimes the only way out is through. The only way to real healing is by being willing to stay." Again, no mud, no lotus.

If you're feeling both stretched and cautiously inspired, believe me, I know just what it feels like to let go of the resentments you've wrapped yourself in for years. It's disorienting to let go of the perfect justification of why you're still holding a grudge over a disagreement or clashing of views that may have happened years ago. Metta for our difficult people is a purification practice at heart. It purifies the mind and the heart of its thick mud, debris, and all that is obscuring us from being able to rest in love, freedom, and peace. When done even a little, you will feel better and your heart will be lighter.

metta transforms negativity

We send metta toward our difficult people—from the ones we never thought we could forgive to our annoying new neighbor who just can't seem to remember to lock the front apartment building door or who plays their music too loud or who always parks in a way that makes our morning reverse that much more difficult. Because the negativity we feel for them—resentment, grief, disappointment, and anger—is actually causing us to suffer greatly, to send kindness to someone who has harmed or hurt us is also a significant act of self-respect and self-care. To start this phase of loving-kindness practice, I suggest you pick one of your "lighter" difficult people first, especially if this is your first time practicing this meditation. The idea is you want to go from your milder cases of difficult people to your most painful ones as you gain experience sending metta in this way.

As we get settled in for meditation, remember to be aware and respectful of your heart's practice edges. It is quite normal to bump right into them when doing this phase of loving-kindness practice! You can always go back to the breath at any time or you can return to sending metta toward yourself or your beloved benefactors. Hold a lot of compassion for yourself in your meditation practice today. I know this isn't easy, but I promise it will be worth it.

---

today's meditation

LOVING-KINDNESS MEDITATION
TOWARD DIFFICULT PEOPLE

- Start by getting comfortable and grounding yourself.
- Allow your attention to settle into your body. Take three deep mindful breaths, as you close your eyes.
- Start to send loving-kindness first toward yourself, repeating your personal metta mantra a few times in your mind.
- Let yourself rest quietly for a moment. When you feel ready, call to mind your difficult person.
- Try to reflect that all beings deserve care, and if at all possible, remember a good quality about this person. If nothing good about them comes to mind, that's okay too. You can simply say their name once in your mind, or visualize them.
- Start to direct your metta toward them now. You can repeat the same phrases you have been sending toward yourself or the following mantras.

metta mantras

*May you know happiness and the roots of happiness.
May you be free from suffering and the roots of
suffering.*

- Continue to send metta toward them, recalling that you can go back to focusing on the breath at any time or to sending metta toward yourself.
- Allow any feelings to be here or arise, as you send wishes to your difficult person.
- Toward the end of your meditation time, let any image of your difficult person dissolve from your mind.
- Take three deep mindful breaths once again.
- At the end of your third exhale, place your hands over your heart, thanking it for its willingness to open up to the inner work of this practice.
- When you're ready, open your eyes.

Sit quietly for a moment and simply notice how your heart is right now. There is no right or wrong when it comes to metta, especially when sending metta toward our difficult ones. Take as much time transitioning from your meditation practice as you need.

When you're ready, pick up your practice journal and move into today's reflection exercise. Write down your difficult person's name or make a list of your difficult people. Once you've written your list, pause, connect to your heart space, take a deep breath, and then journal your thoughts on the following question.

REFLECTION QUESTION: When I offer loving-kindness and compassion to [*name of difficult person*], how do *I* feel?

Jot down any and all insights that arise for you. Make sure to be extra caring with yourself during today's journaling.

TODAY'S METTA MOMENT

When we send metta toward our difficult people, we are not condoning their harmful actions or behaviors. We are working with the pain in our own heart. We are taking responsibility to heal and clean up our own heart so we no longer suffer due to someone else's mistakes or harm they have caused.

If not today, someday soon you may notice you start to feel better or differently toward your difficult people. At a certain point, sending metta toward my mildly and most difficult people gave me this insight: Overall it wasn't worth it to me to hold on to these feelings of negativity anymore. It feels much better to wish them metta on the fly, as needed, when I come face to face with them or when they cross my mind. Continue directing metta toward your list of difficult people today and notice the freedom you too may find.

———

DAY 7

---

dissolving
barriers to love

Love Heals.
—*bell hooks*

YOU'VE DONE A LOT of inner work this week! So as you arrive at Day 7, let's celebrate your work by taking a long, deep, smooth breath and reflecting upon the terrain traversed thus far. You have learned you are worthy of receiving the generosity of your own heart. You have started to become your own BFF (how awesome does that feel!), and you developed self-love and respect. You then extended this loving-kindness to others, to those you know well and not so well—your beloved close friends and family members, your local grocery clerk, the neighbor down the street. And you even started the deep healing work of sending metta toward those who have harmed your heart and caused you pain. This is no small stuff. This is what a commitment to real love and healing looks like. This is you saying yes to life and kindness now. You are fully showing up for your practice. Trust me, it's worth it.

As we land at the end of our first week of the brahma-viharas, recall how their purpose is to train our heart's capacity to meet

71

what is here in a boundless, limitless, and unconditional way. It is in this meeting ground of our awareness and love where we find our true home, "the sublime abiding" as the Buddha says, "freed from hatred and ill-will."[9] It gives us a true taste of the contentment, happiness, and peace many of us have been searching for. Metta reforms us. It asks us to reshape our inner world so we can break free of all the barriers we have constructed around our ability to be and extend love.

At the beginning of the week, you started with you, at ground zero. Today it is time to extend your loving-kindness to all beings everywhere—any sentient being alive in the whole world, without exclusion and preference. The magic of practicing metta is embedded within each intentional wish. You peel back and purify each layer covering your heart's natural ability to share its inherent goodness and kindness to all beings near and far, loved and not-so-loved-yet. The heart is at home in this homeostasis. It is also your authentic resting state of unobstructed love, coupled with unbounded happiness, equanimity, and the ability to rejoice freely in the goodness you see in others. In this state of true love, any barriers to belonging—for ourselves or others—are dissolved. Before meeting metta's melting warmth, our ability to love was obstructed by these layers of separation that clouded the mind and heart with a view that supposes "we are separate." This sense of separation brings us out of alignment and causes so much of our world's suffering, heartache, and pain.

In one of my first metta meditations, I recalled experiencing the liberation and unbounded joy of unbrokenness, inclusiveness, and belonging when I was a little girl roaming my family's backcountry woods and the great shaded pine forests of rural Ohio. During these playful moments I felt in total union with the natural world around me, completely void of feeling broken or separate.

I invite you to pause right now and reflect back to when you've felt profound intrinsic inclusiveness before. Think back to a time free from barriers between you and the loveliness of the natural world, other people, or beings around you. Perhaps this is when you viewed your favorite sunset over a special place on a beach you once visited. Maybe it was on a hiking trail surrounded by the secret silent creaking language of wise oaks trees and sweet young cypress growth. Or as you were breathing the crisp daybreak air while riding up a ski lift to the peak of a beloved mountain, quiet with a new coating of fresh nighttime snow.

Take your practice journal and pen in hand and write down any insights that come up. When was the last time you felt whole, loved, held, seen, and one with the world around you?

metta for all

Dissolving our barriers to love is surrendering any belief systems and story lines of undeservingness and separation. Instead, we choose equality and inclusion, starting with ourselves and then slowly sharing this balanced and peaceful love with others and with the universe at large. At its core, metta is meant for everyone, regardless of species, gender identity, race, or religious beliefs. The universal love found within the very heart of metta meditation shows us our heart's true nature, which is unbiased, unbounded, interconnected, and inclusive. The unified homeostasis of the heart teaches that everyone and everything deserves our love and attention simply for being alive and contributing to the orchestra of organisms living on this earth. Our whole-ism mirrors the holistic nature you were just reflecting upon a moment ago. Here is where you heal the divisions of your heart and mind and step into the immeasurable loving state of freedom and loving awareness for all.

Wishing all beings everywhere genuine happiness, well-being, complete freedom from suffering, and safety from harm is the ultimate expression of the heart's ability for limitless joy and inclusion. Being egalitarian with our love leads to real happiness, and it's *really* fun too, which you'll see for yourself in a minute. This last stage of loving-kindness practice points us to the nondualistic nature of reality and the roots of genuine compassion. Even those who have caused much harm and suffering in the world—I have found a doorway for including them in our metta by wishing them eventual freedom from suffering. Their harm spawns from greed, hatred, delusion, and confusion. To wish them freedom from these root causes of suffering is to practice loving-kindness for all beings, even the greatest of perpetrators.

In our final practice of Week 1, you will extend the strength and vastness of metta by first visualizing a circle of loving-kindness. This inclusive circle of loving-kindness holds you, your beloved benefactors, your neutral people, and your difficult people that you were working with this past week. Remember, it's in the sending of metta toward each person or being in your circle where you will discover any remaining barriers to loving without bias, and you will work to dissolve them. Then you will rest in the real freedom of unbounded metta by expanding your heartfelt wish for all beings everywhere to know the sweet uplift and relief of loving-kindness.

Let's begin your last practice of Week 1!

today's meditation

EQUAL LOVING-KINDNESS FOR ALL BEINGS

- Find your seat for meditation.
- After you close your eyes, take three deep mindful breaths.
- Then as you let the breath settle into its natural flow, recall your inner motivation for incorporating metta into your life. Let it inspire you and make you feel strong and free.
- Since the nature of true love knows no bounds and is equal in its ways, call to mind your circle of loving-kindness. In this circle you see all beings worthy of your love and your heart's undivided attention. This includes you, your beloved benefactor, your neutral person or people, and your difficult person or people.
- Start to send loving-kindness to each being in your circle. Begin with yourself, then move to each person or being until you reach your difficult one. Holding in compassionate awareness, notice how your heart feels and where it remains open or closed.
- Once you send metta toward your difficult person, take a moment to see your circle of loving-kindness—each person there, wishing and wanting to be happy just like you. Each trying in their own ways to be free from their sufferings and pain.
- Begin to expand your well wishing to include all beings everywhere, without exclusion, without preference.
- Start with the beings closest to you, perhaps a bird or car driver you hear out your window. Then widen your circle of metta toward all people and beings on your block, in your

neighborhood, in your town or city, in your country, and in the whole world.

· Allow a wave of metta to emanate from your heart.

· As you rest in this worldwide flow of metta, send metta toward all beings everywhere with the following mantras.

metta mantras

May all beings be happy.
May all beings be healthy and well.
May all beings be free from suffering and difficulty.
May all beings know ease and peace.

· Keep wishing metta toward all beings in the universe until the end of your meditation.

· When you are ready, release the metta mantras and rest in your own being.

· Reflect on your own limitlessness.

· When you're ready, open your eyes.

You may be in a wave and wellspring of liberated heart and connection. You may also be aware of where your metta is still limited—that is okay! Remember, the self-awareness gained through mindfulness goes hand in hand with metta. You must know your edges and to whom, what, and where you are applying your metta.

With this awareness and cultivated spaciousness, take out a pen and your practice journal and start to make notes on the following:

REFLECTION QUESTION 1: How can I be a vehicle of love?

REFLECTION QUESTION 2: How can my love and kindness know no bounds? What barriers of separation can I dissolve to be more limitless and inclusive with my love?

Lean in and write to your heart's content. After you've completed today's reflection, close your eyes, take a deep nourishing breath, and send yourself gratitude. The work you have done this week has allowed you to take the next step in your meditation practice and the first step into the loving home of the heart.

From my heart to yours—welcome home.

TODAY'S METTA MOMENT

Keep any and all insight gained from today's meditation close to your heart as you move into the next present moments of your day. Let your heart flow with metta. Let it ring loudly with the joyful and well-intentioned wish: May all beings, everywhere be happy. May all beings in the whole universe be free from suffering and safe from harm.

When it comes to taking the next step in our meditation practice, I love to reflect on the Pali word for mindfulness, *sati*, which translates as "to remember." When we maintain the recollection of our heart's capacity for unbounded love and compassion, we simultaneously remember our own true nature and homeostasis of the heart. After all, we are the love that we are seeking and working to give. Metta just shows us the way to uncover it and the doorway into this natural existence all beings are born into.

———

TEACHINGS ON COMPASSION

Karuna (compassion), the second of the brahma-viharas, shows us how to live deeply from the heart. In fact, I know of no greater healer, alchemist, and teacher for learning what it truly means to be a heart-based human being other than karuna. It is indeed the way to meet our humanness directly and learn how to navigate the inevitable terrain of heartbreak, difficulty, and pain we all experience during our life spans.

Most simply, compassion is the wish that all beings, including ourselves, be free from suffering. Traditionally, compassion is described as the quivering or trembling of the heart in response to pain and suffering. When I first heard this description, something about "trembling" felt familiar to me. I can recall thinking back to previous times my heart felt moved, quaked, or shattered, such as after receiving news of a past partner's cancer diagnosis well after falling in love with him. I distinctly remember my heart taking in the news like an earthquake's freshly made divide across the earth. Then rumbling pain shook my insides for some very long moments, followed by an open-sore quietness.

The newly acquired wound was just there, aching. Then after a few deep breaths, I was overtaken by a lionhearted, roaring resolve to do anything and everything I possibly could to help support his healing journey. This is how compassion works— what causes our hearts to tremble and crack open becomes our newfound courage and conviction when met with karuna's wise and loving response.

the compassion crossroads

The compassion response can be complex and nuanced though and often requires our conscious moment-to-moment choosing and lionhearted commitment. In order for the heart to be able to respond with this innate empathetic tremble, first we must choose how to relate to the distress, sorrow, and loss that we perceive. I call this the "compassion crossroads," those few long, heart-trembling moments for me when time slowed to a halt and I recognized my deep pain on behalf of my partner as well as my love for him. In retrospect, I can see I chose to face the quaking in my heart because I was already in love; therefore I couldn't turn away from it or walk away.

The first choice you make when you respond with the love of compassion rests in whether you will stay and face the pain and suffering you view or feel or close the shutters to the windows of your heart. The latter is more of a shutting down and an avoidance to take in life's pain and discomfort, which is quite normal until you commit to living from kindness and responding to yourself and the world with compassion, so don't sweat it if you are feeling like you are a classic avoider or find yourself shutting down when you encounter suffering.

It took me many years to warm up to compassion practice. Just the idea of broaching this approach to suffering can make anyone a bit squeamish. Who wants to dwell in pain and sorrow for too long? Who wants to feel bad? Karuna asks us to dig deeper than we may be used to doing and to be willing to face our biggest fears, challenges, and adversities with great clarity and courage. To move toward and bravely face that which causes us pain is the terrain of compassion. And a wild thing happens when we do this, when we go against the grain of our usual way of avoiding life's hardships with apathy, neglect, or outright anger: we feel empowered, awake, and *with* the suffering of the world. Once we bravely open to what normally makes us close down, we are free. Our heart is liberated. We become stronger.

For compassion to really work, we must call upon our mindfulness practice. Compassion is a natural wisdom. It accounts for the causes and conditions of suffering. So to respond with compassion, we must see suffering with clarity and right view. The little bit of nonjudgmental space we get from mindfulness, the practice of creating the pause between stimulus and response, is the groundwork for stepping into compassion. Mindfulness allows us the clarity to know where to apply our compassion. And as you will discover this week, your willingness to turn toward that which causes you discomfort and distress, coupled with the heart's trembling response, informs the mind how to act compassionately and from authenticity.

how to practice

Much like metta, compassion is practiced through the repetition of words and phrases in the mind along with the felt sense of softening and love in the heart. To wish yourself and others "to be free from suffering and the roots of our sufferings" and to be "free from sorrow and pain" will require real bravery and courage. Therefore, the first step of compassion practice is to be willing to face your fear of not feeling good all of the time and to relinquish the urge to avoid being affected by suffering.

We think that if we open and lend our heart to sorrow and pain that we will become overwhelmed, drained, decentered, or swept away by the suffering we see or experience. We think our inner light will be snuffed out—the impact will be too much to bear and the pain will consume us. My student Ashley shared with me, "I'm always afraid to open my heart when I watch the news or scroll on social media after a celebrity's death or national tragedy. It feels so overwhelming. I must be such an empath!" Ashley's experience is not uncommon. Yet when we take a look at compassion intricately and get up close to it in the practice, we see it is really the other response choices at the crossroads of compassion—anger, avoidance, fear, grief, and wishing harm—that have the capacity to overtake us, not being too empathetic or too openhearted.

When our initial inclination is to harden and close our hearts in the face of suffering and we choose instead to open with a compassionate love, we move into the second step of compassion: learning the way of being *with* suffering. This is another way of relating to our adversities and the pains of the world. It just requires us to choose something different, to take the wise road of willingness and be alongside our fellow humans' pain while letting compassion ripen our hearts. Quite honestly, I have come to dearly adore the aging and maturing that compassion leaves upon our weathered and worn hearts. Compassion turns pain into something beautiful and workable if we let it.

KARUNA TOWARD SELF

Meditation is a practice of turning inward and meeting the landscape of our inner terrain. The thoughts, habits of judgment, and stuck emotions we become aware of through our increased self-awareness can be quite painful. What do we do with this new purview into the inner workings of our heart and mind?

How do we handle the shadow-based snapshots of self-data that come up? Or the self-blame, berating, shame, and inner tyranny? The wounded inner child? The piece of our heart still stuck in a relationship from two years ago?

To start, we have the practice of self-compassion, one of the greatest self-healing tools at our ready disposal. The really good news is that while at first glance self-compassion may seem like the most foreign, far-reaching, or unattainable concept, it is actually universal. Why? Because compassion is universal. As you will discover through the course of this week, everyone on this planet is worthy of compassion, including you. You deserve compassion. You also have the inherent right to give yourself the deep healing gift of self-compassion.

KARUNA TOWARD OTHERS

The universal experience of suffering and the universal skillful response to suffering—compassion—are two great connectors we have as human beings. Karuna unites us through our shared experiences of suffering. It says, "Not only do I see you and hear you but I am *with* and *alongside* you. I feel your anguish and I know your pain. Why? Because I have suffered too." Compassion touches all of us on the playing field of life. No one is excluded from these two great connectors. If you are here, breathing and alive in this world, you have experienced mental, emotional, and physical pain in your unique way and therefore you are capable of connecting through compassion with every other single human.

For some, it may be easier to come into contact with compassion by sympathizing with a dear friend's or lover's pain. For others, it may be easiest to think of animals that are suffering in the world and share in their pain. And for others, the easiest doorway into compassion is to live it through compassionate action. As you'll discover this week, one of the vertebrae of compassion is the authentic wish from your own heart to help alleviate the suffering you perceive in the world.

KARUNA TOWARD DIFFICULT PEOPLE

As we practice karuna, inevitably our crossroads of compassion will meet someone for whom it seems rather impossible to feel empathy and good will toward. Whether it is someone who directly caused us harm, annoys us to no end, or caused mass harm in the world, these difficult people cause our hearts to close down and often throw up walls of avoidance or self-protection.

Whenever I am asked about how to extend compassion to those we find difficult, I often think of all the great teachers of the world who have come before me, including Martin Luther King Jr., Nelson Mandela, Mother Teresa, His Holiness the 14th Dalai Lama, and Thich Nhat Hanh. I rest in their noble compassionate hearts and historical actions. They have shown us, by example, how to choose this different way—the way of compassion, the way of healing. What at first conceptually seems impossible (to offer our compassion to those who have caused us or others harm) also shows us exactly where it is that our hearts may be closed. And even if for one far leap of a moment we can open our hearts to our most difficult people and practice offering up a basic understanding of suffering and compassion, while not condoning the harm that has been caused, we can transform suffering while nurturing the possibility of healing, growth, and greater tolerance and acceptance. Then something miraculous happens. We start to feel better and freer while inspiring others to widen their hearts into territories they may have thought unimaginable.

true compassion

True compassion comes from our lived experience. The Buddha's first noble truth—there is suffering and this suffering is unavoidable—boldly lets us in on the true nature of human reality. Once I really opened up to this, I realized the more difficulty I go through, the bigger my heart becomes. As I widen my direct understanding of suffering, I can then offer genuine understanding to others' ignorance, harm, and suffering. This is not to advocate looking for suffering or becoming a martyr of suffering so we can be more compassionate with others. But it does make room for the acceptance that comes when we know that to be human means we will touch suffering, just as we will touch happiness. If anything, this acknowledgment helps us normalize our own suffering a bit more and start to make purpose out of our pain. It gives greater meaning to any suffering we endure. To offer compassion is to stand in another's shoes from our lived experiences. Ultimately, it is the greatest form of saying "me too."

Though this week may seem too heavy to shoulder, remember that compassion is a practice of freedom. It is through acknowledging, holding, and composting our pain that we become stronger and lighter. Each practice this week will introduce you to these principles of compassion in the same reliable way you learned metta.

- On Day 8 you'll meet self-compassion, and you will work with this facet of karuna all the way through Day 10, where you'll begin to bridge your compassion outward to others through forgiveness after spending time practicing one of my favorite meditations for self-forgiveness: the Ho'oponopono Practice for Forgiveness.

- On Day 11, you'll start to open up your flower of compassion to others with a powerful practice meant to guide you to view others and the world through the eyes of compassion. Be prepared to have your world rocked!
- Day 12 will ask you to deconstruct your judgment mind, moving you from judgment and separation to compassion even for your most difficult people.
- Day 13 will bring you to right action—that is, how to live the compassion you feel in your heart in a daily and tangible way.
- And on Day 14, you'll offer your compassion as an act of service to the world through dedicating the merit of your meditation.

To prepare you for this week, I suggest you set the course right now and make a deep commitment to your practice. We are going to dive deep into some uncharted territory of the heart and mind, so make sure to set the intention to be extra gentle, caring, and kind to yourself as you continue to learn how to dwell in the heart through the brahma-vihara of compassion.

DAY 8

---

self-compassion

If your compassion does not
include yourself, it is incomplete.
—Jack Kornfield

HAVE YOU EVER thought about how you fundamentally feel about yourself? If you have, when was the last time you answered this question like you were writing in your adored secret notebook as a child? The kind of notebook that had a brass lock on the side and could solely be opened by the key that you had hidden in the shoebox all the way in the very back right corner of your closet. Or whatever your version of this was! Pause for a moment. Close your eyes. Place your hand on your heart and ask the question again from *this* place. If you have your practice journal handy, go ahead and write down what answers come through.

We start here as karuna prompts us to check in with whether or not we fundamentally feel good about ourselves. When you answered this question honestly, were your answers more on the spectrum of warmth and good vibes toward yourself? Or were your self-sentiments leaning toward coolness, dislike, or bitterness? Sometimes we don't realize the type of feelings we're carrying around about ourselves. This is where self-compassion comes in. Inevitably, once we learn to send ourselves self-compassion, the feeling we have toward ourselves will grow more positive and kinder. Karuna shows us how to value ourselves and know we are worthy and deserving of care and compassion. Because we, too, are human. Regardless of what we've done or not done, or the mistakes we've made, we are deserving of self-compassion.

aversion and avoidance

Two of the main obstacles to self-compassion are aversion and avoidance. That's why I asked you to sit with our question for a moment and answer it as if your answer would be totally safe and secret. Until we give ourselves the respect of honest self-reflection and introspection, we tend to gloss over our answers or only take a sideways peek at them from a distance, all the while continuing to be in some form of avoidance of our deepest truth. My student Jamie puts it this way: "It is so much easier to not take a look at how I'm really feeling. They say ignorance is bliss for a reason!"

It's not easy or comfortable to be radically honest with ourselves. I remember after a period of time well into my meditation practice, I was so let down by all the self-data I was receiving: "Okay, I guess I don't have the highest self-worth after all." "Hmmm, I am pretty direct in all of my personal relationships except in my romantic ones at first. Fascinating . . . (insert exasperated eye roll here)." "Well, I actually don't have the warmest and fuzziest feeling toward myself. Like, at all. In fact, I feel pretty crummy about who I am as an all-around person and human being."

It's important to be on the lookout for these common obstacles to self-compassion. So I have developed a simple three-step approach to giving yourself some karuna even when you feel lost in the woods of avoidance and undeservingness.

THREE SIMPLE STEPS TO SELF-COMPASSION

1. BE WILLING TO SEE YOURSELF CLEARLY. Stop and see your suffering. Pause and acknowledge your feelings. Notice any tendency to shy away from honestly seeing yourself and opening to your truth.

2. MOVE INTO ACCEPTANCE NOW. True self-compassion can only come on the heels of self-acceptance. I love the psychologist Chris Germer's definition of acceptance he uses in his writing and work on self-compassion. He refers to "acceptance" as the conscious choice to experience our sensations, feelings, and thoughts *just as they are*, moment to moment.[10] When we move into real self-acceptance, we're not bypassing or sugarcoating any of our truths that we perceive. Nor are we reaching for any of our usual avoidance tactics, such as numbing out, over- or undereating, watching media, or diverting into our to-do lists. With acceptance we take what we honestly see and we welcome it, opening the doorway to the possibility of self-care, genuine concern, and understanding. More so, acceptance reminds us of an important universal truth we often forget in the face of shame or self-condemnation. Acceptance tells us that it is okay to feel this way and that there is nothing unhuman about how we feel about ourselves.

3. MEET YOURSELF WITH KINDNESS. The third and final ingredient to experiencing self-compassion is when you meet what you honestly accept about yourself with kindness. By doing so, you're choosing kindness over criticism and compassion over judgment.

When you follow these three steps as you encounter the true feelings within your heart and the honest thoughts crossing through your mind in meditation and in daily life, in essence you are reparenting yourself with total compassion. You are developing the inner voice of self-kindness and an inner coach of compassion. Karuna reminds you that every single human makes mistakes, experiences failures, and sometimes makes poor decisions. And it also shows you the way through these human moments by choosing something different, by choosing to change the way you respond to yourself with compassion.

Today you will form and align with your unique self-compassion mantra. Just as you did with your metta mantra last week, you will take it a step further and meet your difficulties and any present self-perceptions with compassion. You will see for yourself how compassion lovingly dismantles all of the old stories we carry unconsciously and makes room for a fresh way of relating to ourselves based on the loving home of the heart.

---

today's meditation

A MEDITATION FOR SELF-COMPASSION

- Allow yourself to be really comfortable for this meditation. See if your posture can be an expression of self-care today.
- Invite in some deep mindful breaths into your body, and when you are ready, softly close your eyes.
- Spend some time resting your awareness in your body.
- As you connect to natural sensations of warmth and ease in your body, place both palms of your hands over your heart, further fostering feelings of warmth and loving care.

- Notice how the state of your body changes when you sense the contact of your palms resting against your heart.
- Silently begin to repeat the following self-compassion mantras.

self-compassion mantras

Dear one,
I see you and I am here for you.
It is okay to feel this way.
May I hold myself in compassion.
May I hold myself in loving care.

- Keep reciting these mantras. Let them reverberate in your heart until you end your meditation.
- Now, reflect on your own personal self-compassion mantra. See if a unique set of words or phrases comes through.
- You can place your self-compassion mantra into a phrase such as: May I _____ (fill in with the heart-based quality that is most meaningful to you. For example, "May I meet myself in a field of loving awareness. May I hold my pain and suffering with tenderness and care. May I acknowledge my true feelings and emotions with respect and total honesty. May I remember the natural strength within me.")
- Close with your hands on your heart. Connect to the warmth and care you've just generated for yourself. And when you're ready, open your eyes.

Pick up your practice journal now and write down your self-compassion mantra (or set of mantras)! This mantra is going to become one of your greatest allies and self-healing tools.

After you've written down your self-compassion mantra, move right into today's reflection question. Take a deep breath, place a hand on your heart, and start to write freely.

REFLECTION QUESTION: How can I meet my unique suffering with understanding and kindness?

Make sure to send yourself some self-love and warmth after today's heart journaling. You are engaging with some real inner work!

COMPASSION IN ACTION

Just like metta, compassion can be practiced in the moment and on the fly. Today your practice is to continue to use any of your self-compassion mantras whenever you think something negative about yourself or notice you are turning away from your feelings. After you recognize these old habits of self-relating, repeat one (or all) of your self-compassion mantras and then add this mantra at the end: "Today I choose something different."

Go ahead and close your eyes for a moment and repeat this to yourself a few times: "Today I choose something different. Today I choose something different." This, my friend, will lead you to real compassionate change and will support you in choosing self-compassion as a new way of living.

Now meet the rest of your day and get ready for the incredible magic that is about to unfold.

——————

DAY 9

---

learning how to
hold your own heart

Our feelings are our most
genuine paths to knowledge.
—Audre Lorde

BEING HUMAN WILL at times break your heart. As the ancient Taoists said, we will all experience the ten thousand
joys and ten thousand sorrows throughout our lifetimes. We
will inevitably bump into heartaches from loss, trauma, grief,
injustice, and anger, whether by our own actions or those of
another. Without the teachings of the heart, we can feel that we
will be lost on the sea of suffering indefinitely at times. Have
you ever felt like this—rudderless, lonely, floundering, head
barely above the water, or even submerged and barely able
to keep up the effort to come up for air? I've been there. The
truth is, we all have, to varying degrees, as I've seen during
my work with meditation students over the years. I have tears
welling from my eyes right now as I recall the countless times
the teachings of the heart have been the only lifeline I could
even fathom to look for, grasp, and then hold on to and how
life-changing it was to realize metta and karuna were the life

preservers I had always been looking for and that, no matter what, they would always be there for me. I remember feeling like I had finally found a lifeboat in the sea of heartbreak and unprocessed hurt and pain that I was holding inside. I began to understand meditation as a place to compost our very experience of human life itself. Through the warmth of the heart and the kind, tender care of sitting with my suffering, I became my own life preserver alongside the teachings. Eventually I learned that I could hold my own heart wrapped up in compassion's strength and love.

saying i am *with* you, i'm here

Compassion points us in the direction of this greater understanding of the brahma-viharas—that is, what it really means to find our way home to living from a state of love. The very definition of *karuna*—"to suffer with"—lets us know that we too, like countless people before us, can learn the way of being *with* suffering—our brokenheartedness, pain, scars, and open wounds. Compassion works particularly in the realm of emotions. This is where I remember first feeling the healing effects of compassion within my heart and mind. It seemed to soothe my most difficult and painful life imprints and emotional residue by acknowledging them with a variety of empathetic warmth I knew I wanted to drink in.

In today's meditation you will learn the exact practice I have used since I became willing to meet my own discomfort, heartbreak, and pain. Compassion gives us the strength to make even our most difficult emotions—fear, anger, anxiety, depression, persistent heaviness of heart—approachable and workable. Even in the aftermath of trauma, natural disaster, pandemic, or divorce, compassion gives us the strength and wisdom to be with our own heart and learn how to hold our own experience with tenderness and care. The emotional freedom we seek from our past or current sufferings happens through meeting ourselves with compassion's wise warmth, to know intrinsically that we are not only capable but also strong enough to hold our deepest emotions and circumstances. This is the heart of self-compassion. Looking square in the middle of our own love and pain while saying, "I am here for you. We've got this, sweetheart. You are strong enough to hold this too."

four steps to your compassion lifeline

Let me describe the steps of our practice a bit before we begin. You'll most likely see the pattern here of starting with mindfulness and then taking the next step into compassion.

Today's meditation is a well-known practice for meeting our most difficult emotions with the transformational qualities of the heart. It is commonly referred to as the RAIN meditation. I know from personal experience, it is just the right mixture of healing and strength that your most painful suffering and sorrow requires.

RAIN is a four-step practice:

Recognize
Allow
Investigate
Nurture

The first two steps, *R* and *A*, are based in mindfulness. Through your mindful awareness you will be able to recognize, acknowledge, and even name your most difficult emotions and then give them the space to be here with you in this present moment through allowance. Allowing is a key step so you don't turn away from these little messengers of self-insight and information or push them out of your awareness. Recognizing and allowing are the bridge between the mind and heart, a true step in chitta—that is, heart-minded consciousness. In step 3, *I*, you will investigate where in the body you are feeling this emotion, and then you will have all of the information you need to apply the heart's nurturing compassion in step four, *N*.

Let's dive right in and give RAIN a try now.

---

today's meditation

HOLDING OUR DIFFICULTIES
WITH COMPASSION

- To start, tune in to your heart and mind as you settle in for today's meditation.
- As you gently close your eyes, place the palms of your hands over your heart, noticing any immediate moods, flavors of feelings, or thoughts present.
- After this initial check-in, go ahead and take three deep, nourishing breaths.
- Let your hands float down gently to your sides.
- As the first step of RAIN meditation is to recognize any obvious or underlying emotions that may be present, for the purpose of this meditation, if there isn't any truly difficult feeling or emotion presenting right now, broaden your awareness to a difficult feeling you have had toward yourself in the past. What feelings do you have (or have you had) that cause judgment, heavyheartedness, or deep distress?
- Do your best to name the emotion you are feeling or working with. Get specific and courageous. No matter what is coming up, see if you can put a label on it, such as "anger," "sadness," "hurt," "anxiety."

- Take a deep breath in and out. Place your hands over your heart and create the space to allow this feeling to be here without averting or pushing it away. This may take a lot of bravery and strength. Or you may feel a deep sense of relief. There isn't any right or wrong way to feel. All you're doing is widening your circle of compassion to include your own heart.

- Let's take this mindful investigation a step further. With your awareness, see if you can investigate where in your body this feeling is presenting itself. Is it living as a squeezing or pressing around the heart? Is it a searing heartache or tender heart heaviness? Is it lower in your diaphragm or tightly held in your abdomen? Perhaps it's the impulse to keep your hands clenched or a tightness in your jaw or shoulders. Go ahead and spend the next few moments scanning your body and investigating where this feeling is presenting in your body.

- Now that you're aware of what you're feeling and you've let it be here with you even for a moment while noticing where in your body this feeling is living, begin to send yourself compassion. Compassion can come through wisdom, love, or a sensation of warmth. It can be through the sentiment of sympathy or the tenderness of empathy. It can be through reciting your self-compassion mantra or by being your own inner compassionate coach, silently consoling yourself with the sweet embrace: "I know, sweet one. I know this hurts. It's okay to feel this way. You will work through this. You are strong."

- Once you've met your difficult feelings with the healing remedy of self-compassion, go ahead and bring your awareness back to the feeling of the palms of your hands pressing against your heart.

- Take a deep breath in and out of your heart space.
- To end your meditation, visualize your heart being held by your hands of compassion. These hands are full of miraculous strength, tenderness, and understanding.
- Stay with this visualization for the rest of your meditation. When you're ready, gently open your eyes.

Right after your meditation, start journaling and capture any insights that came through. Then place your hand back over your heart for a moment, close your eyes, and reflect upon today's contemplation questions.

REFLECTION QUESTION 1: How can I be unconditionally empathetic with my own feelings and suffering?

REFLECTION QUESTION 2: How can I give my emotions the space and compassion they need?

After you've sat with these questions, gently open your eyes and spend the next few minutes journaling your thoughts and answers. Let your pen fly across the page and the words flow. When you're done with your writing, make sure to thank your heart, courage, and strength. You can even place the palms of your hands over your heart again and take one more deep, nourishing heart breath.

COMPASSION IN ACTION

You can return to the RAIN meditation for self-compassion and the visualization of your hands of compassion holding your heart at any time during the day or night. (I even physically place my hand over my heart anytime I need a moment of self-compassion even if it's out in public, such as standing in line at a store!) Be gentle and mindful with yourself for the rest of the day and evening. Make sure to carve out some "you" time. Rest, take a bath, continue to journal your inner revelations and insights, and steer clear of watching a lot of media or engaging with anything too triggering today. Self-compassion is a vulnerable and tenderizing practice, so part of the practice is also being caring and lovingly protective of your heart space.

———

DAY 10

---

forgiveness

Earth is forgiveness school.
It begins with forgiving yourself.
—Anne Lamott

FORGIVENESS IS THE DOORWAY into the unconditional heart. It is both a great healer by way of reconciliation and a practice that will ask for unrequited kindness and compassion at times.

By practicing forgiveness, we are choosing to let go of the pain and stories presently binding our hearts. At the end of the day, forgiveness will make us feel better, less broken, and freer. Not forgiving is the opposite of freedom. When we don't forgive we are not free. This is why we choose the path of forgiveness, even if the reason for our forgiveness seems unworthy of any room in our hearts. Holding on to resentments, grudges, and bitterness harms our internal world and consumes our capacity for inner freedom and openheartedness.

forgiveness is an inside job

An approach to forgiveness I have found helpful from a meditation perspective is choosing to not push anything or anyone out of my heart, including myself. That's the approach I'll introduce to you here. To start, we'll spend time in a meditation on self-forgiveness. Offering forgiveness toward ourselves lays the groundwork for more all-round forgiveness in our lives, particularly toward—you may have guessed it—the past.

Have you ever thought, "I will never be able to let this go or move on; I'm too crushed"? Or "I'll never forgive myself for how I acted toward her; what I said is so unforgivable"? Then self-forgiveness is for you. Self-forgiveness really lets us step into the healing realization that our past does not have to define us. In fact, the core of compassion teachings points us right here to this truth: to place our attention on reality as it is now; to open to the pain, sorrow, and grievances we have endured and collected that have left imprints on our mind and heart and to say, "I see you. I honor you. I know that you are here." When we practice self-forgiveness, we open to the possibility of releasing the boxes and definitions we have put ourselves in because of the past. To forgive ourselves for the ways we have let ourselves down, not acted in the ways we wanted to, or disappointed ourselves in retrospect is to find freedom and liberation from the past in order to step wholeheartedly into the present as our most authentic and loving selves.

For me, forgiveness has been one of my greatest teachers on true healing and reconciliation. There have been two distinct times in my life where I thought forgiveness would be off the table forever. In one of these instances, someone forgave me. In the other, I forgave someone. The through line between these two big teaching moments was that they both took time—months, in fact. And instead of losing patience or faith in the forgiveness process, instead of shutting down to the possibility of moving on in healing, forgiveness came from me and was extended to me with perfect timing. Now in both of these relationships there is great friendship that has deeply enriched my life. For- giveness taught me to not abandon myself or someone else, especially when the sincere responsibility and state of apology was already present. Forgiveness just needed to be given the right space and time.

Much like with metta and karuna, if we have brought our- selves to the awareness that forgiveness is the healing path that will bring us back home to our hearts, we can cultivate the intention to forgive, even if we don't yet feel it genuinely within our hearts. This is where we begin, especially when practicing forgiveness toward someone else. In many ways this is a glaring example of chitta, or heart-minded consciousness. The wisdom in our minds is speaking to the wisdom part of our hearts, lovingly saying, "We both know this is ultimately a good idea. Take your time. Go as slow as you need to. I'm here when you are ready." Compassionate forgiveness is a process. It can take days, months, or decades. You can't force yourself to forgive someone, or someone to forgive you. The blooming of the forgiving heart only happens when it's ready.

PRACTICE NOTE: Just as forgiveness doesn't let us force it, forgiveness does not condone or forget. What may seem unforgivable at first is the very reason we need to practice forgiveness the most. Whatever you avoid forgiving will keep a strong hold over your heart, keeping you from being free to love and to heal. To break through into forgiveness doesn't mean the suffering, trauma, or heartbreak didn't happen. What we are met with is the pinnacle question of forgiveness: How much of this pain, blame, guilt, or shame do I want to carry with me into the present and the future? It's okay to teeter here on this question as long as your heart needs to.

HO'OPONOPONO PRACTICE
FOR FORGIVENESS

When learning about the heart qualities of Buddhist practice, you will start to notice the attention put on cultivating kindness, compassion, joy, and equanimity everywhere, even across different meditation traditions and geographical cultures and within every prominent religion. Today's forgiveness meditation will start with the Ho'oponopono practice for forgiveness, which is derived from the ancestral Hawaiian custom meant to invoke reconciliation, establish harmony, correct wrongdoing, and restore back to order what is out of alignment. Upon first hearing this prayer, I was reminded of traditional forgiveness phrases I learned while studying metta and karuna. These beautiful Ho'oponopono phrases embody where compassion and forgiveness meet.

the ho'oponopono forgiveness practice

I'm sorry.
Forgive me.
Thank you.
I love you.

"I'm sorry" acknowledges what we did that led to pain
    or the mistakes we have made.
"Forgive me" invokes the genuine wish to forgive ourselves.
"Thank you" invites release and letting go.
"I love you" offers the healing of self-compassion.

After you practice the Hoʻoponopono prayer for self-forgiveness, you'll then send forgiveness to someone else. If this is your first time practicing forgiveness meditation, I suggest that you pick a more approachable offender first, much like we did with metta for our difficult people. Then, as you feel ready, you can warm up to forgiving more extreme circumstances. Let's begin.

- Settle your body comfortably into your meditation space.
- Close your eyes while inviting in a deep centering breath through your nose and exhaling through your mouth.
- Spend a few moments resting your attention in your body. When you are ready, begin calling to mind something you'd like to forgive yourself for, whether it be harm you caused to yourself or to someone else.
- Once you've centered your awareness on what you'd like to forgive yourself for, reflect for a moment on the causes and conditions that led to this happening.
- Then bring compassion's wide-open warmth toward whatever emotions and sensations that are arising.
- As you continue to hold this object of forgiveness in compassion, start repeating silently the Hoʻoponopono mantra for healing and forgiveness.

hoʻoponopono forgiveness mantra

I'm sorry.
Forgive me.
Thank you.
I love you.

- Continue to repeat these phrases of forgiveness for as long as desired. Remember, forgiveness can't be rushed or forced. Forgiveness is a natural healing process within the heart with its own timeline and wisdom.
- Once you feel ready to move into the next part of your forgiveness meditation, take a deep, long breath in and out. Place your hands over your heart and thank your heart for the courage and vulnerability it took to send forgiveness and compassion to yourself.
- Then call to mind someone who has caused you harm and suffering.
- Acknowledge what it is they did, said, or didn't do that hurt you. If you can, reflect on the causes and conditions that may have led to their harmful actions.
- Meet your pain and sorrow with the healing balm of compassion. And if your heart feels able, silently send the following phrases of forgiveness to this person or being.

forgiveness mantras toward others

May I forgive you.
May I forgive you today or someday soon.
May I forgive you.

- Repeat these mantras of forgiveness over and over as you hold the circumstances and subject of your forgiveness lightly and compassionately.
- Sending forgiveness toward this person allows you to let go and release your past.
- When you feel complete with your forgiveness meditation, allow these phrases of forgiveness to dissolve from your mind.

- Place your hands over your heart again and hold your tender sweet heart in compassion.
- Take a few deep cleansing breaths, and when you are ready, open your eyes.

Today's reflection questions can be done right now or later in your day, when you've had time to process your feelings and thoughts from the forgiveness meditation. When you are ready, rest your attention lovingly and compassionately in your heart space and answer these contemplation questions.

REFLECTION QUESTION 1: Where in my life can I offer forgiveness?

REFLECTION QUESTION 2: What from my past am I willing to let go of and release today?

After you're done journaling, make sure to pause and thank your brave forgiving heart. You can even silently say, "Thank you, heart, for guiding me to forgive."

COMPASSION IN ACTION

Since forgiveness is a purification practice, be sure to be extra caring and compassionate with yourself today. Your heart may feel cracked open, raw, tender, or vulnerable. You may feel unclear or even confused about your present feelings on forgiveness. Honor yourself by holding exactly where you are at with compassion.

You may also feel relieved, clearer, and lighter from today's forgiveness practice. Perhaps you experienced a healing release or feel freer than you've felt in years. If this is how you feel, I encourage you to make a forgiveness vow—a way to move forward with integrating your newfound forgiveness into the fabric of your being and who you are today. Vow to live your forgiveness through some kind of actionable quality or tangible self-purpose statement.

Write this forgiveness vow down in your practice journal, whether it is to never allow the kind of harm you endured to happen to you again, or to express your own self-forgiveness for the harm you caused by vowing to live in a certain way moving forward.

DAY 11

---

we've all been there

To develop this mind state of compassion,
the second of the brahma-viharas, is to learn
to live, as the Buddha put it, with sympathy
for all living beings, without exception.
—*Sharon Salzberg*

TO THIS DAY, the Buddha's first teachings he gave after his awakening poignantly sum up our human experience. Known as the Four Noble Truths, they give us insight into how to make sense of what we endure and persevere through. In the first noble truth, he expresses that to be human is to suffer. In the second noble truth, he gives us areas to look for that are the causes of our suffering. And then by the third and fourth noble truths, we discover, yes, there is suffering *and* there is also a way through to the cessation of suffering. Compassion, to me, is awakened by resting in these truths of our human reality and humbly understanding that while there is suffering, there is a way to work with it and heal through it.

We are all connected by our capacity to suffer and to heal from suffering. We all suffer. To cultivate an open heart, to stand trembling but strong in response to suffering—our own and that of others—is indeed noble. The Tibetan word for compassion is *nyingie*, translating in English to "noble heart." This way of relating to the world, to others, and to where they too are in the path of the Four Noble Truths is to hold others' own process with respect, nobility, and compassion. We suffer, and we can choose to heal through compassion: as mentioned earlier, these are the two great connectors of our human experience.

I invite you to pause for a moment, place your hands over your heart, and acknowledge the feelings that are here with you now around meeting yourself with compassion these past few days. Is there relief? Is there tenderness? Rawness? Hope? Is there healing? Are there wounds still asking to be held and worked with? Whatever sensations you are aware of right now, in this very next moment I want you to remember that you are not alone with these feelings and experiences. Compassion asks us to get on the playing field of life and be in the messy experience of being human with others. The moment we can touch our own humanness, imperfections, heartache, and pain with understanding is the very same moment that we can automatically start to contact genuine compassion for others. Just as we learn to let ourselves off the hook for being human, we can also learn to let others be in their messy process of humanity. Compassion connects us. It reminds us that we are part of the greater sea of human experience.

see through the eyes of compassion

Being able to offer others compassion comes from knowing and acknowledging our own shadows and demons. We are all capable of causing harm, intentionally and unintentionally. Lifting the veil on our capacity to think and behave unwisely, out of fear or distress, gives us the firm ground on which to relate to humanity—others' misguided steps or actions—with compassionate eyes and heart: "Just like me, you have suffered. Just like me, you are suffering." Just like me, this impatient person in front of me in line is under the influence of stress. Just like me, this person who is honking their horn in traffic behind me is feeling helpless and not in control. Walking down the streets of my neighborhood, I pass a quiet man, contemplative and seemingly withdrawn, and I think, "Just like me, he wants to be free of suffering, sadness, and pain. Just like me, he wants to be happy and supported by limitless love."

This practice has radically changed my way of relating to others and the world. Each time I notice I am about to judge someone or feel sorry for them for saying or doing something embarrassing, I immediately think of a time I did what they did, acted how they acted, or felt how I perceive they are feeling. In an instant I am back in compassion. I see myself in the people around me. If there is one practice I wish for us modern meditators to take on, it might be this. By practicing compassion, we are training to see others as not so different from ourselves and to discover just how interconnected we all are. In the course of every human life, each person will smile and cry, love and lose, grieve and laugh. Karuna asks us to make a little more room in our hearts for others' humanness. This is the start of creating an inner compassionate stance to meet the world: "Just like me, you want to know love and be happy. Just like me, you have caused harm. And just like me, you are longing, unconsciously or consciously, to feel free."

Today's practice is the Just Like Me compassion meditation, which will guide you to meet others with the eyes and heart of compassion. May this meditation change your world, as it has mine. May it lift the illusion of separation and indifference, apathy or social blindness. As you see others through the eyes of compassion—particularly neutral people, those you may not know so well—may you train your heart to cultivate unbiased and genuine care for others.

---

today's meditation

JUST LIKE ME

- Settle into your meditation space.
- Sense your body landing and arriving. Become more aware of your sitting bones, glutes, sides of your legs, ankles, and feet resting against the cushion, ground, or seat beneath you.
- Take a number of deep breaths—in through your nose and out through your nose or mouth—as you softly close your eyes.
- For the next few moments, place your attention on the natural sensations of the breath, one rhythmic outflow and inflow at a time.
- When you feel ready, start to bring to mind someone you know well and rather personally—a close friend, partner, or family member.
- Picture their face, eyes, cheeks, arms, and hands. See them as if they were sitting before you right now.
- Then silently repeat in your mind the following mantra.

just like me compassion mantras

Just like me, you want to be happy.
Just like me, you want to be safe from harm.
Just like me, you want to be free from pain and sorrow.
Just like me, you want to be free from suffering.

- Keep repeating these phrases of compassion, generating an understanding response to their wish to also be happy and free from suffering, just like you.
- If at any time you sense a closing down, anchor your attention back in the breath and begin again when you are ready.
- Allow the image of this person to dissolve from your mind's eye now.
- Call to mind and heart a neutral person in your life. Maybe this is someone you saw at the store yesterday or walked by on the street. Or maybe it's the person who delivers your mail or hands you your morning cup of coffee throughout the week.
- Bring an image of them to mind and repeat the same compassion mantras toward them now.

Just like me, you want to be happy.
Just like me, you want to be safe from harm.
Just like me, you want to be free from pain and sorrow.
Just like me, you want to be free from suffering.

- Stay with this more neutral person for a period of time. Notice if you feel more connected to their basic desire to feel good and free from hardship and difficulty.
- Then, just like before, let the image of them dissolve from your mind's eye.
- Finally, think of someone who you have witnessed suffering recently. This can be someone you know well or not at all. Maybe they were angry, upset, frustrated, or impatient. Or maybe you witnessed them during a moment of embarrassment or doing something not in integrity.
- Repeat the compassion mantras for connection.

Just like me, you want to be happy.

Just like me, you want to be safe from harm.

Just like me, you want to be free from pain and sorrow.

Just like me, you want to be free from suffering.

- For the next few moments, let yourself rest in this expression of shared humanness.
- Now take a few deep compassion-filled breaths.
- When you are ready, open your eyes.

This meditation can be a real eye and heart opener. Whether you feel awakened by this meditation or are still in the compassion-building process, honor the inner work you just went through and recognize you have stretched your heart's ability to connect through compassion.

Today's reflection question can be done right now or later today. Sometimes it is most effective to sit with these reflection questions as you move through your day, and even notice what comes up as you actively live the questions.

REFLECTION QUESTION: To whom else can I offer my compassion today?

Don't be afraid to let your heart stretch and connect today! When you are ready to journal with today's contemplation, make sure to take a deep breath, connect to your heart space, and then let the words begin to fly onto the page.

COMPASSION IN ACTION

You may have guessed it already, or perhaps your natural understanding of these practices is starting to kick in and become more confident. Just Like Me is a profound practice to bring with you out into your day. Without exception, see if you can see the world through the eyes of compassion and relate to others with a heart full of karuna by recognizing all of the ways others are just like you, navigating this oh-so-human experience. Today, each time you see someone doing something that you might have previously judged as right or wrong, or good or bad, note to yourself, "Just like me, this person [*or insert their name if you know it*] wants to be _____ [*insert feeling, emotion or quality of the heart*].

———

DAY 12

---

unconditional love

We cultivate compassion for the
suffering of all the cries of the world.
—DaRa Williams

WHAT DOES IT MEAN to make the heart a home, a safe dwelling place not only for yourself but for others and the inflow and outflow of the world's happenings? Homemaking in the heart starts with a deep excavation, uprooting what is blocking us from the natural resting state of the heart, which is love. This isn't the regular dependent love hinged on external circumstances or our personal preferences that reside in the realm of pleasantness and likeness, as you began to discover when practicing metta. This is an all-encompassing and embracing love. It's an all-inclusive love that truly understands and expands the heart's call to not only choose something different (the way of love) but also to do something different in response to the world's cries of suffering. In this realm of compassion, the opposite choice of love is separation, and for many people, separation stems from judgment. It's the judgment mind within all of us that splinters us into separation.

The good news is, just as metta is the antidote to fear, compassion is the antidote to judgment. It asks us to come to an honest reconciliation with our thoughts, opinions, and preferences. It asks us to take an extensive look at the roots of our thoughts and actions and to dismantle our ways of viewing others and the world as above, below, better than, or less than us.

Compassion is a radical practice in this way. Within it lies the ripe propensity to shake our preconceived notions and sense of self to their core. For many, it may even be a bit disorienting and explosive, especially when we take the step of offering compassion to our enemies and difficult people, as we'll aim to do today in our meditation. Compassion challenges us and our capacity to love. It unearths the biases, prejudices, and limitations in our minds that keep us from standing in another's shoes. Like metta, karuna allows us to examine our judgments and the roots of our judgments, and even our internal and external systematic biases that are often inherited from society and our family upbringings.

Seeing my judgment mind with the eyes of love and understanding spawned a deep deconstructing of my internal viewpoints and preconceived notions I had about others. The experience of deconditioning my mind has been both alarming and liberating, but most of all humbling. I really attribute cultivating an inner compassionate stance as a way to relate to others with a deep-seated state of grace, humility, and porousness. This stance is where we tap into our unbounded ability to love others without the borders of judgment and prejudice.

I know how hard it is. The honest truth is, this realm of compassion is often a terrain of the heart only understood once you have practiced it—like really practiced it. Students of mine often ask me, "But, Amanda, how can I offer compassion to this political leader I despise? Or to the injustice I see all around me? Or to those who put others in harm's way?" These days, my response is, "Compassion really is the only option. If we don't choose compassion, the world will never have the opportunity to grow and change." To be unconditional with our compassion brings us to the very essence of an awakened loving heart—boundlessness; not limited by thinking constructed from preferences and judgment.

In today's practice you will work on generating compassion for those people or entities you judge and find rather bothersome or unfathomably difficult. You'll also work with a series of contemplations that are meant to dismantle your judgment mind, adapted from the revolutionary work of the teacher and luminary Byron Katie.[11] Start where you are, and let this be a great opportunity to not judge yourself in any way! Compassion and forgiveness take time. Sometimes we are simply not ready to stand in another's shoes completely, and that's okay. The mere aspiration is always where we begin, which also has the long-term capability to transform our hearts and minds.

---

today's meditation

EXAMINING THE JUDGMENT MIND

- Go ahead and find a posture for today's meditation.
- Right away, take a long, deep inhale and exhale. Though compassion may feel like a lot of work or heavy lifting at times, it's in this heart work where you will begin to feel clearer, more loving, and freer.
- Take two more deep breaths in through your nose and out through your nose or mouth.
- Then gently close your eyes and rest your attention in your body.

- Guide your attention back to the sensation of the breath. Let the breath become your anchor, the home base for your attention through the rest of today's meditation.
- Spend five to ten minutes practicing breath awareness and becoming aware of when your attention floats into thinking.

When you notice you are paying attention to thoughts in your mind, pause and ask yourself the following questions:

Is this thought a judgment in any way? If it is, move onto the next contemplation. If it's not kindly, guide your attention back to your natural breathing.

If it's a judgment thought, ask, Where is this judgment coming from? Examine if the judgment is coming from a mental idea or a perception. Often these mental constructs derive from the realms of opinion, preference, or belief system, known as your inner biases. Spend as much time as you need to in this contemplation to get to a root cause.

Once you're aware of where your judgment is coming from, gently ask yourself: Is this true? Is this based in reality? Can I let this go? Who would I be without this belief and judgment? Rest in this contemplation for as long as you need to.

Once you feel your judgment's hold on your mind and heart start to lessen, meet that moment with a deep breath and the inner warmth of acknowledgment.

- Repeat this practice with any other judgments you might have become aware of, all the while being very compassionate and kind with yourself in this process.
- Now we'll move into a compassion practice for someone you find difficult or whom you have judged in the past.

- Allow this person (or persons) to come to mind. Notice any sensations in your body, mind, and heart.
- Remembering that you can go back to following the breath at any time in this meditation, start to send them phrases of compassion.

compassion mantras for difficult people and those who have caused harm

May you be free from suffering and the root causes of suffering.
May you be free from ignorance and confusion.

- Send your difficult person these phrases of compassion three more times.
- It's okay if it doesn't feel genuine right now. You are planting the seed for a judgment-free mind and heart.
- Let the image or feeling of this person begin to dissolve.
- Come back home to your heart and breathing.
- Do you sense any inner freedom from wishing this difficult person to be free from suffering?
- Invite in one more deep breath.
- When you are ready, open your eyes.

Uprooting our blocks to compassion and love is what reminds us of our basic interconnected and shared human experience. While our judgments may even be right, to free ourselves from their influence is what helps us to learn how to love more unconditionally. The true nature of love is without discrimination. Compassion teaches us that our happiness and way of relating to the world is in our hands. This alone is enough to liberate our inner and outer worlds.

When you're ready, grab your practice journal and settle into today's heart writing.

REFLECTION QUESTION 1: Where do I have unconscious bias?

REFLECTION QUESTION 2: What healing comes from including my perceived enemies and most difficult of people in my circle of compassion?

PRACTICE NOTE: Deconstructing our internal and implicit biases can be uncomfortable and humbling. Therefore I want you to be sure to counter any feelings of guilt or fatigue with a good dose of self-compassion as needed. You can refer back to Days 8 and 9 for some on-the-spot compassion care, or take solace in knowing these practice edges, though uncomfortable, are leading you to immeasurable growth.

COMPASSION IN ACTION

Working with the judgment mind is a continuing practice from which we can learn so much about ourselves. And through the gentle release of compassion we choose love instead. Today and moving forward, I invite you to take on this illuminating practice. If and when you become aware that you are judging, call your judgment out by noting out loud or silently in your mind, "Judgment thought" or "Judging." Then ask yourself the honest questions, "Is this true? Can I choose to see this through the eyes of love instead?"

———

DAY 13

---

right action

Our practice is homeopathic. A few "drops" of us
devoted to a wise path with heart is massively potent,
and it is this radiance that nurtures our belonging.
—*Ruth King*

COMPASSION STIRS the heart, shaking it out of the status quo
and business as usual in order to meet the suffering we see in
the world or within ourselves. When compassion takes on the
energetic form of action, change and transformation can happen overnight. It's like waking up from a spell of delusion or a
cloudy slumber. Once our eyes open to the pain of the world,
it becomes our heart's job to skillfully guide us in the right
response to what we see.

From the thoughts I have (hello, judgment mind), to weighing
my decisions based on what aligns with my personal values and
mindful living principles, to contemplating not only the reasons
or intentions behind my behaviors but the possible impact *any* of
my actions will have upon others—compassion has asked me to
thoroughly consider my way of moving through the world. Compassion helps me evaluate the words I type in an email, the tone
in a text, whether or not I pause and ask a grocery store clerk,

"How are you today?" It guides me to stand up against racial discrimination, classism, gender inequality, or heterosexism. Compassionate right action asks each of us to get clear on the right view around these topics of moral behavior; integrity; and personal, social, and political values. It asks us to establish our own code of ethics. If we haven't spent time evaluating our own guidelines of personal conduct—what we consider to be right or wrong, or in meditation terms, wholesome or unwholesome—then more often than not we may not be as able to move into compassionate action in a clear-sighted or timely way.

let go of being busy and pity

Along with wanting to weigh our personal values and integrity, we look to right action from the wish to outwardly help others who are suffering. For some, the only way compassion practice feels relevant and real is to express our heartfelt response to injustice or pain through tangible action. For others, practicing compassion through action is a doorway into the compassionate loving abode of the heart. Karuna fosters the heart's wish to alleviate the suffering we see in the world; to help others be free from their physical, mental, and emotional pain; and to lighten their sorrows.

When we contemplate right action and wholesome responding, compassion can also express itself by moving us out of indifference. We realize the unethical thing to do is to be silent and complacent around any injustice or suffering we see. Compassion helps us draw our movements, words, and speech from a place of impassioned concern. We need to address any suffering we see; we no longer can be bystanders, waiting for someone else to be the first one to pledge care. I remember my mentor, meditation teacher Mark Coleman, saying this on a retreat I attended with him: "A block to responding with compassion is our 'busyness' or pity for another."[12] Before we develop a compassion-based inner response system, we may see the suffering of others yet dismiss it because we are putting our own agendas, self-perceived safety, or happiness first. Or we may think there is something wrong with them, so they deserve our pity instead of help.

be in alignment with right action

A way to bring compassion to life is by practicing a mindful living principle: do no harm. By "no harm," I mean as little as possible to zero harm at all through our speech, actions, and behaviors. The Buddhist moral practice of taking the Five Precepts—abstaining from killing, stealing, speaking falsely, nonloving sexual behavior, and intoxicants—is how we can train our hearts and minds to do no harm and to stand for love. I started working with these well-tested guidelines when my meditation practice developed to a point where I had the intense desire to do as little harm as I possibly could in the world. All of the little manipulations of truth, trying to sway others to see my way, and being self-protective or dishonest really didn't work for me anymore. Years before I had also given up alcohol and all intoxicants, period. Looking back on this decision now, I can see how it was one of my own initiations into practicing right action and nonharm in my unique way while also making a stand for love and healing.

building your inner compassion compass

One of the things I love about aligning ourselves with compassion through actionable response is it shows our reverent understanding of interconnectedness. By mapping out our integral values, choosing our ethical views, and taking steps to alleviate another's pain and suffering, our right action becomes a love language, expressing itself through solidarity and a willingness to provide relief in the face of suffering.

All of our actions can be based in love. In fact, every single ordinary daily action can be laced with the healing medicine of compassion: practicing deep listening; sitting with another, holding their hands and heart; practicing deep breathing for a moment to regain our own sense of inner ground and resta-bilize our compassionate stance. Sometimes, simply sharing our presence with another and being there as they are going through difficulty is the most medicinal form of compassion. These are all ways our compassion can take the form of action and become a natural way of responding to the countless human moments of suffering we will see in the world.

To bring your authentic compassion to action, I often rec-ommend following what stirs and moves your heart, especially in direct response to suffering and pain. Perhaps this means using your voice or influence to express what is unwholesome to you on behalf of others. Maybe it's setting the boundary for the final time, saying, "Enough. I will not allow this to happen ever again." Compassion is a strong energy when it takes the form of action and impact. Today, the world needs you and me to stand in solidarity with love more than ever before. Get ready for your meditation today, as it is a practice designed to guide you in learning how your heart is stirred and living from your heart's compassionate responses.

---

today's meditation

NOTICING WHEN THE HEART IS STIRRED

In this meditation, you will bring your mindful recognition to what stirs your heart in response to perceived injustice, sorrow, or pain. You'll also notice if your heart is moved by qualities of happiness as well. The main purpose is to form a direct connection to your heart's quiver so you can then move into action from there.

- Find your seat in your meditation space today.
- Invite your body to settle into a posture that feels nourishing, supportive, and full of ease.
- Take a few deep breaths in and out.
- When you're ready, gently close your eyes.
- Guide your awareness to your heart space.
- After a few moments, reflect back to the last time you felt called into action for a deeper reason or cause.
- Bring this instance to mind and for a moment remember some of the details that ended up igniting you into response.
- Notice how your heart feels now. Is there movement and energy?
- If your heart's response is due to witnessing a moment of pain or hardship, take a deep breath in and out and continue to bravely explore how your heart responds.
- Now, allow another memory to come to mind—a previous moment you were equally called to respond with great spirit and swiftness.
- Notice how your heart feels now. The heart is a message center of great wisdom and right action. It recognizes love in an instant and can guide you in the right direction.
- Continue this practice for the remaining time in meditation, contemplating how your heart stirs in response to what it witnesses.
- When you're ready, end your meditation with a deep breath in and out.
- Slowly open your eyes.

Move right into action after this meditation. Lift up your practice journal and start writing your heart's response to today's reflection questions.

REFLECTION QUESTION 1: To where and with whom can I bring compassion into action?

REFLECTION QUESTION 2: Where may I be withholding my compassionate response?

Let the words flow onto the page. This *is* your compassion in action. Don't stop writing until you've emptied out all of these life-affirming insights from your meditation practice.

COMPASSION IN ACTION

Today I want you to further reflect on your practice journal responses. Then take these insights and answers into action by making a commitment to compassionate action!

Perhaps your compassion in action is through a daily moment of showing care like we discussed, such as kindly listening to a friend or family member's worries with nonjudgment and an open heart. Or maybe it's picking up the phone and calling your local congressperson to ask for a change you've been wanting to see happen! True compassion will call upon your heart to step into action and create change. Be willing to bring your compassion to the front lines of your mind and heart, stand firm in your authentic values and moral compass, and follow through on what you deeply know to be wholesome and in the name of love.

———

DAY 14

---

dedicating merit

But compassion isn't about solutions.
It's about giving all the love that you've got.
—Cheryl Strayed

AS YOU CLOSE OUT your week of incredible excavating compassion practice, I honor your heart's journey these past seven days. If there is one thing I hope you take away from this book, it's this: meditation is a practice you do not only for your own benefit but also on behalf of others and the world. The shifts in your heart and consciousness become about how you show up in your life and what you stand for. Your kindness, compassion, joy, and equanimity can touch the hearts of others.

At the end of every meditation class, I tend to reference this in some way, shape, or form. If you've sat with me in a class or at a speaking event, you probably know our ending instructions really well at this point: "Now as you float open your eyes, pause for a moment and choose to bring the qualities of mind and heart you cultivated during your time in meditation out with you into the rest of your day and share them with the world." This perspective will make any and all uncovering or discomfort you went through this past week worth it, I promise. After all the time on the cushion working with your own mind and uprooting blocks to love in your heart, now it's time to share your work.

This shift from me to we in meditation is a powerful one. In fact, it can be a great motivator for your practice, and it often quells common concerns of newer meditators that all of their minutes on the meditation cushion are self-serving only. Through learning how to make your meditation practice an offering not only to yourself but to all beings everywhere, your engagement with mindfulness and the heart practices turns into a flowering gift, nourishing countless beings in the world.

it's not about me anymore

Recently I was looking through old practice notes I often scribble down when I'm in a meditation class or retreat with teachers in my meditation lineage. As I was shuffling through lined notebook papers with insights and teachings captured over a weeklong meditation retreat, my eyes landed on a little personal note to myself written off in the right corner on a page. It read, "It's not about me anymore. It was, I admit. But now I just want to be a vehicle of practice for others." My practice had turned from my personal desire for more happiness and well-being to one of service, and cultivating these qualities within me so they could be of benefit to others.

After this retreat, I started to study what is known in Buddhist framework as the bodhisattva's way. What I love about this teaching is it marries the heartfelt wish for our practice to be of benefit to all with the heart quality of compassion. In essence, a bodhisattva is someone who is devoted to waking up and practicing for the benefit of all sentient beings through living with compassion and with the welfare of others in mind.

To practice with this bodhisattva aspiration is to let your practice become a force of healing in the world. Your everyday actions, thoughts, and speech turn into opportunities to practice with this great wish for all beings to be free from suffering and to know happiness and the roots of happiness. You remove the blocks that prevent you from relating to others with kindness and compassion so all beings can know the healing fruits of metta and karuna. You dedicate your practice so all beings can experience the medicinal freedom derived from unconditional love, care, and concern for the welfare of their hearts.

In today's practice I will guide you in a simple dedication meditation, one you can end your periods of personal practice with from this day forward, if you feel inspired to do so. This bodhisattva aspiration is much like a flower. It will bloom over time when the conditions are ripe and ready. To dedicate "the merit" of your meditation is to share any value, benefit, or goodness gained during your practice with others and all beings, unconditionally and without exception, which fosters a generosity of the heart and spirit. Over time you may find that this sharing of your practice makes you feel good—and even happier. The teachings of the bodhisattva show us our inherent interconnectedness in this way. The more generous we are with our presence, kindness, and compassion, the happier we become in the long run, as you will discover in our next week of practice together when we spend time in the third loving abode of the heart—appreciative joy.

To further prepare you to dedicate the merit of your practice, may these words from His Holiness the 14th Dalai Lama speak to the seeds of generosity within you already. His interpretation of the Bodhisattva Prayer from Shantideva, a sixteenth-century practitioner who channeled the teachings of the bodhisattva's way and vows, always bring me back to my deepest of intentions—that is, to be a vehicle of practice for others and the world. May these aspirations inspire you too:

> May I be a guard for those who need protection
> A guide for those on the path
> A boat, a raft, a bridge for those who wish to
>   cross the flood
> May I be a lamp in the darkness
> A resting place for the weary
> A healing medicine for all who are sick
> A vase of plenty, a tree of miracles
> And for the boundless multitudes of living beings
> May I bring sustenance and awakening
> Enduring like the earth and sky
> Until all beings are freed from sorrow
> And all are awakened.[13]

Before you begin today's practice period, pause for a moment and reflect upon who you might want to send a little bit of your practice to today. Maybe a family member has been suffering or unwell, or a beloved friend could use some support and uplift. It's okay if no specific person or being comes to mind right now. You'll have time to contemplate the recipients of your meditation's fruit at the end of today's practice.

today's meditation

DEDICATING THE MERIT OF YOUR MEDITATION

- Settle into your meditation space.
- When you are ready, take a few deep centering breaths and allow your eyes to gently close.

- Since we are at the end of Week 2, I invite you to do a little self-guided practice to start with today.
- You can spend the first portion of your meditation settling into your body and then place your attention upon the sensations of the breath for a period of breath awareness.
- Then choose one of this week's compassion mantras—whether it be a phrase of self-compassion or forgiveness—that resonated with you or one that you could use a little bit more of in your life today. Or choose a set of compassion phrases you feel inspired to send to someone else. Trust your inner wisdom and let any words be the perfect phrase to practice with today.
- When you're ready to bring today's meditation to a close, before you end, dedicate the merit and any goodness gained during your practice.
- First, contemplate any specific being or persons you'd like to send the merit of your practice to.
- With them in mind and heart, silently say the following mantra.

dedicating merit mantra

May the fruits and benefits of my practice bring
peace and happiness to your heart today.

- Now you'll generate the authentic wish for your practice to be of benefit to all beings everywhere without exception.

dedicating merit to all beings mantras

May my practice be of benefit to all beings.
May any merit from my meditation reach the hearts
of all beings everywhere.

- Spend a moment resting in this heartfelt aspiration for all beings everywhere to benefit from this time in meditation.
- When you are ready, take a closing breath in and out and softly open your eyes.

Pause for a moment and contemplate how your practice can be of benefit and serve the world around you today. Know that you and your practice have become strong enough to hold all of your own pain and heartache. Your dedication to let your practice be for others is a beautiful expression of compassion that will bring much-needed healing, relief, and happiness to all who are touched by the fruits from your meditation.

My hope is that you feel good about all of the heart work you've done this past week! Compassion gives us ample opportunity to grow our capacity to be strong in the face of adversity and keep our hearts open to the world. In turn, we spread a type of reassurance and wish that all beings be free from suffering and know the happiness and peace within their own hearts.

Before you start the rest of your day, spend a moment with your practice journal and jot down your thoughts on today's reflection questions.

REFLECTION QUESTION 1: What is one act of kindness I can give today?

REFLECTION QUESTION 2: How I can turn my practice into an offering that I can share?

COMPASSION IN ACTION

Let these final reflection questions from Week 2 be the way you share your practice with the world today! Know that the fulfillment of your happiness and joy comes from being a loving refuge for the well-being of others. Your compassion assignment is to share one act of kindness today and let your practice be a dedication to everyone you interact with.

———

TEACHINGS ON APPRECIATIVE JOY

Mudita is the medicine known as joy. It's the third pillar of the loving heart and a rather special kind of joy, one that has the ability to make great shifts and changes in your life. Coming off of your week practicing compassion, you may be wondering how on earth you are going to switch gears into a quality of the heart that asks you to rejoice and take delight in life. Well, as you will find out over the next seven days, the brahma-viharas reflect the true nature of life itself.

Just as there is a path through life's hardest moments, which metta and karuna show us how to meet so well, there is also an abundance of goodness in our lives to take delight in, as mudita reminds us. Joy and happiness are intertwined in the fabric of life itself. Mudita gives us the insight on how to touch into the sweet happiness of being human, the uplift we feel when we see good happening in the world, fall in love, or have a dream come true that we've so dearly wanted. Mudita teaches us how to take notice of these moments, our own inner goodness, and the good-heartedness of others and to celebrate happiness when it is here. Joy balances compassion and loving-kindness. It points us toward *sukha*, "life's sweetness," even when we know we will always encounter *dukkha*, "life's suffering," as well.

Translated from Pali Sanskrit, *mudita* means "sympathetic joy." If you take a look at the root word for *mudita* in Pali, it means "to be pleased" or "to feel gladness," particularly in the mind. As you are doing with all four brahma-viharas, you are training an aspect of chitta, heart-minded consciousness, toward being unobstructed in your ability to love.

Mudita is the path for developing a joyful mind, and one of the best ways Buddhists have found to awaken natural joy is by rejoicing not only in our own happiness but in *other* people's happiness as well. That's right, a doorway into living a joyful life, a happy existence, and a gladdened mind is by celebrating others' success and good fortune—a seemingly tall order at first, yet so incredibly helpful and liberating when done. For this reason, mudita is also referred to as altruistic joy, empathetic joy, vicarious joy, and appreciative joy, just to name a few. This particular flavor of joy can eradicate some of our most common and painful modern ailments, such as joy guilt, comparing mind, envy, spite, jealousy, resentment, judgment mind, and any stinginess with selective celebrating, which are often all brought to light through our relationships and how we relate to other people—namely, our friends, not-so-much friends, coworkers, or even strangers on social media.

Mudita is so radical in this way, as it is completely dependent on us choosing to celebrate the good and take notice of our genuine good-hearted intentions for ourselves and others, whether we think we want them to be happy or not! I have grown to love mudita practice for this very reason. No matter how far down I get on the jealousy road or how many plots I come up with to make sure I will get the very exact outcome my mind has fabricated or fantasized or decided that I need no matter what, mudita always cuts down my ego talk in an instant. It is one of the quickest ways I have found in my seventeen years of meditation practice to return to love.

In our week together, we will call mudita "appreciative joy," as I feel it points most directly to the essential qualities of joy that make it easier to really feel happy for others—even toward those we don't particularly care for or like. As you will learn on Day 19, appreciative joy can be encapsulated in one simple phrase: regardless of who you are or what I think of you, your happiness makes me happy. Mudita teaches us the more generous we are with our love and celebration of others, the happier we will feel and the more joyful we will become.

how to practice

Joy is an intentional practice. So often our minds are running on autopilot when it comes to happiness, with all-too-familiar story lines. Have you ever thought, "I'll feel good when I get that new cute fall jacket or finally get this work project done" or "I'll be happy when I have a certain amount of money in my bank account" or "I'll be happy when I have a specific number of followers on social media or get recognized in my career"? We can unearth these grooves in our brains with the intention to show up in joy and rejoice for others. The Buddha talks a lot about joy for this reason. Why? Mudita gives us a way to dismantle the usual habit loops of negativity and closemindedness and do something different, something more life-affirming and expansive. Responding with joy can activate a host of more wholesome alternatives, such as meeting our own greatest hits of comparing, competitive, and envy-filled mind with the antidote of noticing what is working in our lives and what brings us joy, as well as finding happiness and delight in other people's good fortune. Most wonderfully, choosing joy takes the sting out of hearing or seeing our usual triggers! We'll be talking more about this on Day 16.

MUDITA TOWARD SELF: REJOICING IN YOUR OWN HAPPINESS

To cultivate appreciative joy, you must first touch down into the boundless joy available to you in your own life. Thich Nhat Hanh says, "How can we feel joy for another person when we do not feel joy for ourselves? Joy is for everyone."[14] Awakening to your own joy can be as simple as taking delight in a gorgeous blooming flower, hearing the sound of your beloved's voice, or noticing the way your favorite song soothes your heart. Waking up to your own joy asks you to investigate your past and present relationship with what brings you happiness and joy. As you will find out, there are many different flavors to joy. Dr. Paul Ekman, a world-recognized emotions researcher at the University of San Francisco, California, writes that joy can be expressed through a variety of ways.

Here are some of the ways to joy from his list:

The pleasure of the five senses—like taking a lick of
    your favorite ice cream flavor or seeing a beautiful
    sunset
Amusement and humor—the felt-sense experience of
    your own laughter after a healing joke
Contentment—a subtle satisfaction where you are
    relaxed and at ease
Excitement—the most intense kind of joy in response
    to novelty or change

Relief—the feeling after a strong emotion occurs and
then subsides

Wonder—the enjoyable feeling of being overwhelmed
by the incomprehensible

Ecstasy or bliss—a high frequency form of joy, a state
of self-transcendent rapture

Exultation—the feeling following the completion of a
great challenge or difficult task

Radiant pride—when someone you love experiences a
special moment of success

Schadenfreude—unhealthy relishing in someone else's
suffering

Elevation—"the warm, uplifting feeling that people
experience when they see unexpected acts of
human goodness, kindness, and compassion."[15]

Gratitude—the appreciation of a selfless act that you
may have benefited from[16]

Matthieu Ricard, the cellular geneticist turned Buddhist monk,
has added three more facets of joy to this list: rejoicing—in
someone else's happiness (a main component of our work together this week); delight or enchantment—a shining kind of
contentment; and spiritual radiance—a serene joy born from
deep well-being and benevolence.[17]

When we start to open up to the ways in which we feel joy,
we realize that joy is so often readily available at our fingertips.
Even when we are at rock bottom or within a spell of depression,
to train the mind in joy means we take notice and attend to just
how joy may still be present amid our darkest of moments. In
this way, joy becomes a subtle way back to the fundamental
pleasure that's always there in the present moment.

MUDITA TOWARD OTHERS: REJOICING IN OTHERS' HAPPINESS

Appreciative joy lets us relish other people's success, good fortune, and what makes them happy. When we practice mudita, we take delight in everything virtuous that makes them smile while tracking our own heart's response to their gladness. Right away, when we take in another's happiness as our own and do a happy dance on their behalf, we will most often be able to tell whether it is an authentic happy trot or one that is a bit forced and performative. This is the rich territory in celebrating others' joy and happiness. It highlights where our heart is closed in sincerely wanting the seeds of happiness for this other person to keep growing and bearing fruit. Therefore, appreciative joy helps us overcome a plethora of unhelpful mind states particularly in our relationships with others. Whether feeling spite or resentment, wanting to control just how much success one person should experience in a week, or feeling jealous or competitive, we free the tight hold negativity has on our mind and heart the moment we go into practicing happiness for someone we feel any of these feelings toward.

Throughout this week, you are going to uproot these painful mind states and work with them by wishing yourself and others happiness and joy, as well as expand your heart's capacity to feel and receive joy.

- On Day 15 you'll focus on what brings you joy and how to let go of any guilt you may feel about being happy.
- On Day 16 you will start exploring joy through appreciation and gratitude, a major theme for the week.

- The meditation on Day 17 will shift your world as you practice working with the ego to release any unwholesome negative mind states you have toward others.
- Then from Day 18 onward, you will practice appreciative joy by widening your circle of rejoicing beyond your current inner circle of besties or others that look and behave like you, beyond your implicit preferences and biases, to letting joy become a vehicle for recognizing other people's basic goodness.
- On Day 21, you will meditate on true celebration, really rooting for others' success while feeling the effects of limitless appreciative joy in your heart.

It has been said that appreciative joy is the most difficult of the brahma-viharas to wrap our heads around, let alone really take on as a practice. In many ways, mudita runs against the grain of how many of us have grown up in Western culture. We have been taught that there is only so much love, money, resources, and happiness to go around, and if we don't protect our slice of the prosperity pie, our good fortune will be taken from us, like pirates hunting treasure.

My commitment to you over the next seven days is to grow your ability to rejoice while touching down in contentment, rapture, and real happiness. I want you to unapologetically feel all of the abundance joy has to offer and learn how to meet the world around you in radiant delight and unconditional love. By signing on to this training in kindness by bringing this book home with you and making it to this very page, ultimately you are learning just how much joy, healing, and relief the authentic sharing of your kindheartedness brings to the world.

DAY 15

---

the seeds of
genuine happiness

Don't miss it!
—James Baraz

DURING THE SPRING OF 2015, in Dharamshala, India, a highly anticipated meeting in the theological and spiritual worlds took place. His Holiness the 14th Dalai Lama of Tibet met with Desmond Tutu, the archbishop emeritus of South Africa. During these dialogues, the Dalai Lama reminded audience members of his view that the very purpose of life is discovering happiness and exploring joy. Further along into their days of discussion, the Dalai Lama and the archbishop, along with Thupten Jinpa, His Holiness's translator, shared an important distinction between how happiness and joy are experienced: Joy is something different than happiness. Happiness is experienced much of the time as a feeling in the body through sense pleasures or based on external stimuli. While a deeper level of happiness can be experienced "through our mind, such as through love, compassion, and generosity. What categorizes happiness at this deeper level is the sense of fulfillment that you experience."[18] Whereas "joy is our essential nature, something everyone can realize. We could say that our desire for happiness is, in a way, an attempt to rediscover our original state of mind."[19]

To practice mudita for yourself and others is to undertake joy as a training to find your way back to this original state of mind. The mind can be primed for joy. It can be taught how to lean toward joy and take on a growth perspective, ultimately leading to joy and happiness for everyone involved. When you start looking for the seeds of your own happiness, you don't have to look too far, as joy will tell you. With this shift in perspective, you will be prompted by joy to ask some very precise questions: "What else is there? Is this it? What can I learn from this experience? How can I shift my perspective to a positive one? How can I contact peace in my heart?"

I had the timely pleasure of having a private small-group audience with the Buddhist teacher and joy expert James Baraz a few days prior to writing this section of *Kindness Now*. Over the two-hour-long talk he gave on his book *Awakening Joy*, he kept repeating a wise yet rather mischievously inviting phrase when telling us how to awaken joy in our lives. He would say, "Don't miss it. Don't miss it!" The art of training the mind in joy and tapping into the seeds of genuine happiness is to be mindful of all the joy at our disposal and to pay attention to the natural wonders of joy. As you learned in this week's introduction, joy is expressed in at least fifteen different ways. So really, to cultivate joy is to say yes to paying attention and remaining awake in our lives, *in a certain way*, with intention and in a way that is authentic to you.

joy is available now

It is our job as practitioners to pay attention to these cracks of light and love no matter what situation we may be in. Whether we are anxious, jobless, alone, or bereaved, we seek balance by remembering the nature of our human existence. There will always be joy and sorrow rotating as guests at our door. The living, breathing questions then become: How do we navigate these experiences? What wisdom can be gained? Where is there love in this sorrow? I've bumped into these questions during my daily life experiences. When I'm feeling off or self-critical and the sound of a hummingbird reaches my ears, I take natural delight in the red-throated bird's chirps. Or even recently, I woke up to a foggy coastal day in Los Angeles when the weather forecast predicted blazing-hot summer temperatures. I savored the coolness of the ocean breezes against my skin. When we rest in and appreciate the small things in the present moment, we can get in contact with the essence of joy. Then we can let these small daily moments remind us that every moment holds joy. We can train our minds to relish and rejoice in any of these flavors and expressions of joy in the pressing spirit of "Don't miss it!" By intentionally recognizing happiness and joy, we start to awaken to a level of profound authenticity. Through the active practice of seeing the world through the eyes of joy, we align with the natural hum and rhythm of life itself.

WHAT TO DO WITH JOY GUILT

Since today is our first day of Week 3, I want to address a main obstacle I see to feeling authentically happy and at home within our joy. When talking about happiness, many of my students share these common sentiments: "I just don't feel like I deserve this" or "I feel bad about being happy, especially when there is so much suffering and unrest in the world." I'm going to suggest you pause and reflect on the following questions: What is your current relationship with happiness? How do you react when you read the word *happiness*? Take a moment and jot down any immediate thoughts and insights in your practice journal so you can be mindful of your present happiness baseline.

As mentioned before, joy is the original state of the human mind, and happiness is very much our untouched state of sensed fulfillment. Both joy and happiness are our birthrights. Through meditation we get closer and closer to who we really are, before all of the layers of conditioning set in and we started to wear the burdens of stress. Just keeping this simple truth in the background of your awareness is a solid starting point whenever you notice yourself questioning your right to feel happy and joyful. Much like wishing yourself the heartfelt wish of happiness, health, kindness, and freedom from suffering when practicing loving-kindness and compassion, you're meant to feel the fullness of happiness when it's here and the spark of joy from something sensational, benevolent, and pleasant. There just really isn't any other way around it. So even when you think you don't want to feel happy or you have guilt for riding on the wings of joy for days on end, take a step back and rest in the basic human aptitude to feel whole, complete, happy, and free. Wear your joy unabashedly and radiate your fundamental happiness without limit or a second guess.

---

today's meditation

WHAT BRINGS ME JOY?

For our meditation today, you are going to begin to create your new habit of recognizing what miracles of joy you have available to you right here in this moment.

- Start to settle in.
- Take a few natural breaths.

- Softly close your eyes.
- Spend these next few moments scanning your body with a gentle warmth and tender care.
- Lightly guide your attention to the natural inflow and outflow of the breath. Let any thoughts cross through your mind, smiling at them if that feels helpful, and release them one by one.
- Now center your attention in your heart and start to ask today's mudita mantra.

mudita mantra

What brings me joy?

- Wait for the answer. Recognize it. Relish it. And ask again: "What brings me joy?"
- Notice the blessing of joy that comes to mind. Recognize it, savor it, then repeat again, "What brings me joy?"
- Keep repeating the mantra and reflecting on all the ordinary and extraordinary occurrences that bring you joy.
- Give yourself permission to feel good and see your life through the eyes of joy.
- Continue this practice until you feel complete.
- When you are ready, open your eyes.

Go ahead and grab your practice journal right away! Your reflection practice today is to write down the full list of what brings you joy. I encourage you to keep reaching for as much joy as possible. Let this list of joy elevate your mind and heart.

TODAY'S MUDITA MOMENT

A very powerful practice to further flex your joy muscle in day-to-day moments is to actively train in diversifying your joy.

Often we are more primed in one to two flavors of joy, such as the experience of sensory pleasures or the great gratification of exultation. Today, take a look at the list you just wrote of what currently brings you joy and take note of your main ways of accessing happiness, joy, and fulfillment. Then refer back to the introduction of Week 3 and the list of different ways joy is expressed. See if you feel drawn to experience joy in an area you might not normally. Also, don't sweat it if you have a really action-packed day today. You can also simplify this mudita moment by continuing to notice what brings you joy.

———

DAY 16

---

a direct lifeline
to the heart

Rapture is not a selfish emotion. It is pure gratitude,
flowing freely through the body, heart, and soul.
—Elizabeth Lesser

TODAY YOU WILL EXPLORE another primary obstacle to appreciative joy. This roadblock to real joy and happiness can be major, so I've allocated a whole day for you to be able to recognize it when you see it and come back to your good-hearted intentions for joy immediately. Are you ready? Let's dive in.

Jealousy and comparison are two modern-day epidemics. Regardless of your age or social status, these two poisonous mind states are all pervasive, sparing no one. After any time spent on social media or in a peer-oriented work environment, it is easy to see that the struggle with envy and conceit are real. Both jealousy and comparison invoke a primitive part of our brains, based on methods of survival,[20] and induce a common human characteristic of competition. We are wired to want to win, at all costs and even at the expense of others. Of course, the choice to practice the brahma-viharas gives us a way out. Thank goodness for these direct antidotes to two of our biggest modern pain points! It's okay if you want to take a deep breath in and out here. I, too, feel relieved from just reading these words on the page.

jealousy and comparison

It's important to understand these two opposites to genuine joy and happiness in order for you to apply a skillful response without delay. Appreciative joy practiced toward those whom I have compared myself to or felt jealous of has literally saved my sanity more times than I can count. Jealousy (envy) and comparison (conceit) make us lose our centers and any self-reference we have based on inner equanimity. The moment we judge, compare, and oppose anyone's good fortune or success, we start to derive our identities from how we think we stack up against them. "Well, they have more friends and followers than me, so they must be more popular and likeable. On the other hand, it looks like I have more money than they do. Okay, maybe I am not as beneath them as I initially thought."

Jealousy and comparison lead to incessant measuring and assessing, completely undercutting our joy and happiness. Not only do we lose our sense of center in who we really are but also our thoughts, speech, and behavior become based in reaction to all of the suffering we feel. These two obstacles pose a real threat to our ability to rejoice in others' success, happiness, social status, or number of friends and followers, and are very painful and all consuming. Jealousy becomes like a relentless thrashing in the mind as it tries to assert itself over the people we are envious of. And comparison tortures our spirits. It's like we are in crazy town and become unrecognizable even to ourselves.

Most alarming, when the mind is filled with jealousy and constant comparison, it triggers some of our deepest wounds as spiritual seekers: destructiveness and lack—namely, we don't have enough, or worse, we are not enough. When we are operating from this constricted shadow-based place—if jealousy and comparing minds go unchecked in the unconscious—it can become really easy to do great harm. These highly afflictive states hijack our executive functioning and evenmindedness and cripple our inner goodness. Have you ever had the thought, "It would be so much easier if she didn't even exist. Then I would be so much happier!" Or have you ever planned out six different strategies to show up your nearest adversary or enemy? "If I undermine their intelligence, or just move their backpack so they can't find their year-end presentation before our final class today, then I'll be able to show how much better I am than them. Then I will feel happier."

You might have noticed one of the ways to joy listed in the introductory pages to our week in mudita is called schadenfreude, the German word for the unhealthy relishing of someone else's suffering, embarrassment, or diminishing. This confused perception leads us to think that we will feel better if the ones we resent have their talent, success, or happiness done away with all together. The veils of jealousy and comparison make us feel separate and are based in illusion. From the Buddhist perspective, all greed and envy—the stories we spin, the tales we construct, the webs of pain we cloud our hearts in—are based in delusion. The truth is, when we hurt others, we simultaneously hurt ourselves. The Buddha shares a parable of a person holding a hot coal ready to be lobbed at their near enemies. As you can imagine, before the coal is thrown it burns the hand of the person holding it.

gratitude is a direct lifeline to joy

Gratitude and mindful appreciation are a potent treatment for envy and comparing mind. It brings us back to center and reminds us of all the good that makes up our lives: "Oh, I have this goodness happening over here for me in my life! I have my health. I have my inner circle of friends whom I trust and adore." Gratitude guides us back to our original mind and true nature. It is a great ally of joy and can be a direct lifeline back home to the heart. It leads to the ability to live from your heart instead of solely from your mind. When you live from the heart, there's not much room to be spiteful, vengeful, or jealous. It's only when you live from the mind that you have the propensity to act from a place of smallness and lack. Becoming heart-based is the way of the brahma-viharas. When you are heart-centered, you know the value of rejoicing in the success of others who trigger you and practicing gratitude for what you do have and all of the abundance in your life.

Today's meditation will be on coming into contact with your grateful heart. Get ready to step into appreciative joy.

today's meditation

GRATITUDE MEDITATION

- Let your body come into a comfortable position, then take a nice nourishing breath in and out and close your eyes.
- Gently begin to invite your body to soften.
- Scan your body in a kindhearted way.
- Guide your attention to the rhythms of the breath now.
- And as you keep a light connection with your breathing, begin to reflect on the following contemplation.

mudita mantra

What am I grateful for?

- Witness what comes up for you. Savor this gratitude, and ask again, "What am I grateful for?"
- Perhaps a totally different gratitude comes forth or the same gratitude as before. Pause. Savor. Appreciate. Then ask again, "What am I grateful for?"
- Keep reaching for the next gratitude and then the next one, until your whole mind and heart are filled with loving appreciation.
- Embrace all of the sensations from your gratitude and spend the next few moments resting in this state of gratitude.
- To close, invite in a deep refreshing breath and release this breath out.
- Slowly open your eyes.

It's time for some gratitude journaling in your practice journal! One of my favorite post-meditation practices is to write down a list of my daily gratitudes. I hope you find as much fulfillment from this exercise as I have over the years. If you haven't done so already, pick up your pen or pencil and start writing down your gratitudes that came up in meditation and any more that you want to appreciate! After you write your list of gratitudes, end this journal practice by closing your eyes, placing your hand on your heart, and appreciating all the reasons you have to be grateful. You can keep this grateful heart with you as you move through the rest of your day.

TODAY'S MUDITA MOMENT

Now that you are filled up with gratitude, you're going to keep working with appreciative joy by practicing mudita for anyone who triggers you, anyone for whom you feel jealousy, and anyone you feel compelled to compare yourself to today. When you are aware of yourself judging or feeling resentful or envious, take a mindful breath and see if you can practice being happy for them. Find *any reason at all* to rejoice for them, no matter how big or small. Then follow up this practice with remembering your own list of gratitudes from your meditation today and feel yourself returning to your home base within the heart.

———

DAY 17

---

letting go of the ego

This is not mine, this am I not, this is not myself.
—*Samyutta Nikaya*

THE FOUR BRAHMA-VIHARAS are abodes of true love. Again and again without fail, when any of the four qualities are invoked, in that very instant we begin our return to love. Of course, if we find ourselves returning to love, that most likely means we were out of alignment with our true loving nature. What causes us to veer out from love, you might ask? On one hand, the answer is simple: anything that separates us from our loving heart, anything that pulls us out from our home of love. On the other hand, to honestly view the reasons we become separated from love is much more complex. The moment we choose to look at these reasons behind this separation, we are in fact coming face to face with our very own ego—a pivotal part of the meditator's path.

meet the ego

The ego can be a real barricade to kindness and love. It constructs itself on the opposites of love. It builds upon fear, self-protection, illusion, jealousy, judgment, and anything negative that pulls us

157

out of love. Not to worry, though. Self-awareness is our greatest asset when it comes to working with the ego. The ego likes to operate undetected in the subconscious, and bringing our conscious awareness to the ego is what starts to heal our separations from being a heart-based human.

Learning the characteristics, tactics, and behaviors of your ego is the way you return back home to your loving heart. To do so, you must be willing to let go of all of the pleasing, building up, boosting, coddling, and pacifying your ego gives you. Your ego is your defense mechanism to the deep-rooted discomfort of being vulnerable, alive with the world, and openhearted. In other words, your ego likes to keep you pleased and comfortable by creating a story about the "I" and "the other." For instance, when you're in your "I," you have power, control, and autonomy with "my house," "my boyfriend," "my business," "my car," "my feelings," and on and on. When your "I" is threatened—let's say, if your landlord raises the rent on you, your boyfriend or girlfriend doesn't show affection exactly as you would like, your business has a few setbacks, or someone else gets the new car you wish you had—these small little ego bruises create the illusion of "the other." Then it will create some really juicy stories about these others, assigning labels around "liking and disliking," "better than or less than," "friend or foe." Soon your ego's opinions and judgments have created a pretty fixed view on these others. For example, have you ever wanted to list all of the reasons your current crush should choose you over the other person they are dating? Or how you deserve to get the apartment you want more than the other three applicants who most likely want it just as bad as you? Most of the time, the ego stories are not only not real but are also based on the past or the future. They pit you against the others, along with all the stories you created about those others in your mind.

Your ego's hold over your boundless, compassionate, loving nature will begin to dissolve the moment you place your awareness in the present and commit to learning these habits of the ego. This really is the work of a lifetime. Egolessness is synonymous with true happiness and freedom. To learn to let go of the ego becomes your way to real interconnectedness and authenticity. The ego's negativity will no longer be running the show.

LETTING GO OF SELFING

One of the main tools to build your awareness of the ego's illusions is to look for what I like to call "all of the selfing" going on. This selfing is the hallmark of ego pain, centering, and wounding. When you notice any of the following, you can witness the ego at play:

Self-righteousness—the need to assert your view over
    others
Self-reference—your reality as based on identities and
    constructed self-personifications
Self-centeredness—your worldview is self-focused
Self-importance—the perception that you are better
    than or above others
Self-interest—operating out of self-serving motivations

Once you're aware of these ego tactics, the next step is to take a breath, conjure kindness, and let all the selfing go by actively releasing the ego-based thought or perception from the mind. The moment you become aware of your ego, you weaken its hold and then can actively let go by choosing to return back to love. The ego's web of negativity is what keeps us from feeling good, a part of the world, and free flowing. It blocks us from our genuine ability to rejoice for other people and take part in their happiness. The less ego, the more space, kindness, thoughtfulness, consideration of others' welfare, patience, and compassion we have to occupy our minds and hearts.

And really, the more you know your own ego, the more you will be able to witness it in the people around you, so you can practice compassion on the spot as needed, which will also bring you back to love. The more in touch with who you are, the more you are able to know others. These seemingly small moments are all miracles of potential—the moment you drop your stories and false perceptions, you will start to feel better and instantly happier. Don't worry, today's mudita moment will be this very practice, so you will have plenty of opportunities to further explore this for yourself. Plus, in today's meditation I will be guiding you through this very process.

Ready? Let's begin.

today's meditation

LETTING GO OF THE EGO

- Settle into your meditation space. Breathe in and out.
- When ready, close your eyes.
- Let your awareness slowly scan your body, softening any tension you may notice.
- Then guide your attention to your in-breath and out-breath. Keep your attention focused on your nourishing breath for the next few moments.
- Now I want you to reflect back to the last time you felt negativity toward someone else. This may have been due to something they said or did, or because of a certain opinion

you formed about them. Spend some time focusing in on this instant, and as you remember, your mind may go back to a more negative mind state or feeling. That's okay. Let yourself feel these emotions and sensations for a moment. And further, see if you can gain clarity on how your ego was at play. Was it judging? Assessing? Self-centering? Being defensive or unkind?

• Once you've witnessed any egocentric moves, take a deep breath in and out . . . release any ego views or perceptions from your mind.

• You can even silently say the following mantra.

letting go of ego mantra

Thank you, ego. I am choosing love today.

• Guide your attention back to your heart space and cultivate kindness for the next moment or two.

• Recenter yourself in your loving home in the heart.

• Breathe in this loving nature.

• Breathe out real love.

• Practice this a few more times until you get the hang of these steps.

Witness your ego.
Release its views.
Take a deep breath.
Return to kindness and love in your heart space.

• As you revisit the judgment-free zone of your heart again and again, notice how you may feel more at ease and better each time you return home to your loving heart.

- When you are ready to bring this time in meditation to a close, place your hands over your heart and send gratitude toward your inner wisdom for helping you become more heart-centered today.
- And open your eyes.

When you choose to let go of the ego and return to the home base of love within your heart, true happiness and love flourish. By releasing your ego's constructs, you start to move from being me-minded to we-minded. You see yourself in others, from their happiness to their confusion, and within their joy to their pain. With this view you can transform separation into interdependence while perpetuating unconditional love.

You can choose to do your contemplation practice right now or before bed tonight after you've had some more time to practice this exercise. Feel into what is in alignment with you. If you had a major insight during today's reading or meditation, I would suggest moving into this reflection now.

When you are ready, open your practice journal and freewrite on today's post-practice contemplation:

REFLECTION QUESTION: Where in my life can I move into a state of love instead of negativity?

Make sure to be extra kind and caring with yourself during this honest reflection. Remember, letting go of the ego is the work of a lifetime and may be brand-new to you! That's why today's mudita moment is here for reinforcement. Know that each time you practice witnessing and releasing your ego, you are growing your ability to let love lead the way.

TODAY'S MUDITA MOMENT

Alright, you know the work meant for you today! I promise, by letting go of your ego, you will become freer and freer to feel authentically happy for yourself and others. Let's review your steps toward egolessness one more time.

- Anytime you sense your ego trying to assert, distort, or control (see selfing list above again to know what to look out for), witness your ego.
- Release the ego-oriented thought or perception (you can even send it a mental farewell note like you did in today's meditation).
- Practice mindful breathing.
- Choose love, and recenter yourself in your heart space.
- Affirm that you want to view and interact with the world from this place of love.

I'm so excited for you. This is a big step in your practice path. May it support you deeply.

———

DAY 18

---

widening your
circle of joy

Our top priority is a happy life.
Build a happy individual.
Happy family. Happy society.
And ultimately, a happy humanity.
—*His Holiness the 14th Dalai Lama*

HAPPINESS, RAPTURE, appreciative joy, and pleasure can become a way in which we engage with the world. Mudita becomes the energy and frequency of which we interact with our friends, close loved ones, coworkers, and fellow human beings. The living question when practicing appreciative joy becomes, "Can I take delight in what is causing them to smile? Can I be genuinely happy for them?" Rejoicing in others' good fortune aligns us with the infinite potential of human happiness. The more we look for happiness, the more we will find it. The more we notice it, the more we come to know the innate capacity all beings have to feel joyful. Then our circle of joy has the potential to expand.

joy for miles

Many years ago, I was in Boston, Massachusetts, at a contemplative science conference where for three whole days, the world's leading scientists and Buddhist scholars gathered together to talk about the cutting-edge research being conducted on meditation. His Holiness the 14th Dalai Lama was present to host a master dialogue with some of the researchers. It was a truly rare public appearance for him in the US, and many viewed this opportunity to be in the same room with him as a gift of a lifetime. Conference attendees lined up for hours before the session with His Holiness began. Outside, crowds of practicing Buddhists from across the East Coast formed in hopes of catching a glimpse of their beloved spiritual leader and possibly exchange a bow as he was escorted inside the conference hall. I was there representing the research team I was a part of at the time. We had contributed a scientific finding from one of our studies on meditation, and I was there to answer questions and share about the research study.

The morning of His Holiness's appearance and conference address, I heard murmurs running through the crowd that the energy of the building just felt different to them that morning. Of course, there was the buzz and excitement of hundreds of Buddhists gathering outside, news channel TV cameras to document the occasion, and the secret service there to ensure His Holiness's safety. As his master dialogue neared, I recalled hearing a fellow researcher say offhandedly once that the radius of a holy person's kindness and enlightenment can be felt for many miles around the very location they presently stand upon. I remember thinking to myself, "Where's the scientific proof for that statement? What a bold remark to make." Yet being the rather empathetic and sensitive person that I am, I couldn't help but notice that the energy did feel different. There was a sense of uplift, serenity, and wakefulness present, as though a subtle joyful peace was starting to cloak the hallways and conference rooms. Even as people waited in line for coffee before the keynote address, their faces seemed happy and pleased.

As I noticed the mood shift and change the morning of His Holiness's dialogue, I found myself thinking back to what the fellow researcher had said, and I found my heart feeling warmed and happier by this notion; that all of us—each and every individual, whether a reporter, a security guard, a bird perched on the roof outside above us, a café worker, a scientist, or a lifelong Buddhist monk—were feeling the effects of the Dalai Lama's years of practice, his hard-earned joy and happiness, his great virtue and symbolism of what he meant to an immeasurable number of people across the world.

The truth is, I felt the presence of such practice there that morning and as he spoke to the hundreds who had waited in line to gain access to his conversation with the neuroscientists Dr. Richard Davidson and Dr. Amishi Jha. Whether the many-mile radius has ever been scientifically validated became less important to me. To this day, I still find myself relishing this concept that our individual circle of joy can ripple out and reach all the beings around us. Mudita reminds us that joy, happiness, and freedom from suffering are for everyone. And our hearts recognize these qualities in each other. The goodness in my heart feels the goodness in your heart. Liberation knows liberation. Happiness knows happiness. Joy knows joy.

In today's meditation, you will further strengthen your muscle of love and appreciative joy through practicing gratitude for others. Gratitude is such a bridge builder between our hearts and the hearts of others. It helps us train our ability to look for, take note in, and even reflect back others' goodness. Valuing the goodness we see, the goodness from others we receive, the goodness we generously share with those who enter our field—be it a foot, a mile, or a full radius of many miles around us—paves the way for a life committed to sharing the joy we have come to know in any way we can. Whether through a smile, a comforting hand on someone's shoulder, or even an enthusiastic comment about the weather, whatever way you can share a unique expression of joy without prejudice with those around you expands the field of love in the world. In many ways it is our responsibility to genuinely divvy out joy whenever we can.

When it becomes difficult to feel joyful for someone else, the doorway in can be to contemplate a reason, no matter how big or small, to appreciate them. Research on gratitude has shown that it blocks negative emotions such as envy, resentment, depression, and regret and boosts our feelings of happiness.[21] This is why gratitude behaves as such a strong ally to joy. Even a little flavor of appreciation can point the mind in the direction of seeing joy.

---

today's meditation

APPRECIATING OTHERS

- Take a long deep breath in and out as you settle into your posture for today's meditation.
- When you are ready, close your eyes.
- Start to scan your body, sending appreciation to your body.
- Then guide your attention to the breath and spend the next few minutes letting the breath lead the way.
- Now begin to reflect upon someone or some being that you feel grateful for today. This can be someone or some being that you know well, like someone close to you or your loving pet.

- Reflect upon any specific reason you are grateful for them. This can be for some help, love, or support they have given to you in some way.
- Notice how feeling grateful for them softens your body even more and warms your heart. Your face may relax. Your shoulders may drop. You may feel an overwhelming sense of appreciation for how much they mean to you in your life.
- Then silently thank them in your mind and feel the goodness of your heart sending them this thanks.
- Pick another person or being to feel grateful for. Repeat the same practice with them.
- Continue to locate who you are grateful for and send gratitude to each.
- To end today's gratitude meditation, picture each person or being you felt grateful for as if they were sitting in a circle right before you.
- Feel their presence and beautiful hearts. Rest in their goodness and the goodness that is naturally reflected within you.
- To close, invite in a deep breath in and out before you open your eyes.

Training in mudita is a meeting ground for both your mindful awareness and the seeds of happiness in your heart. Guiding your mind to gratitude encourages the heart to open with joy. For today's reflection, create a list of who you are grateful for and the reasons why you are grateful for them. Then savor and notice all of the appreciative joy swelling in your heart.

TODAY'S MUDITA MOMENT

Mudita is a very relatable practice. When you spark joy in another's life you instantly feel closer to them and share in their smile, happiness, or the appreciation they feel for you! Look for ways to share joy today. This can be through complimenting someone or shouting out the good deed you just witnessed them do. When others feel seen and appreciated by you, their happiness grows, which in turn makes you feel happy too! Be a mirror of joy today, happily sharing your appreciation for others and the goodness you see around you.

———

DAY 19

———

your happiness
makes me happy

All the joy the world contains
Has come through wishing happiness for others.
—Shantideva[22]

A COUPLE OF YEARS AGO I was in New York City getting ready to teach a workshop on the brahma-viharas. The day of the talk, I headed to the part of the city where the workshop was being held to settle in and review my outline and meditations one last time before teaching to that evening's audience. After locating the venue, I found a coffee shop right around the corner that looked bright, spacious, and inviting. "What a perfect place to get ready for tonight!" I thought to myself. As I walked in and took my place in line to order, I realized just how busy it was inside. Being right in the heart of New York City, every single inch of table space seemed to be accounted for and each seat occupied. Whenever I am in situations where the odds don't necessarily seem in my favor, I tend to practice mindful breathing and be optimistically open to seeing what happens. With this spirit, I waited in line, warmly greeted the barista, made him smile and laugh as he took my order, and then turned around to see still not one single seat had opened up. Standing for a moment, I noticed how there were a few café tables and a big community table. The community table was packed practically shoulder to shoulder, so I found myself thinking, "It would be really ideal if one of those small café tables opened up."

My tea was ready at the counter, and right as I scooped it up I saw someone standing up getting ready to go, leaving open a spot at the communal table. "Well, this is better than not having a place to sit and prepare," I thought. So I walked over to the cozy seat between two other New Yorkers, strategically placed myself and my things down between them, our elbows brushing up against each other. I began maneuvering my workshop notes out of my bag, and right as I placed them down on the table I saw a man who had been in line right behind me sit down at a spacious empty seat—one of the very seats I had been eyeing and hoping to set up at, as it had its own small café-sized table all to itself. It was an even more perfect place for me to feel comfortable for the next few hours before having to head over for the talk.

Feeling a tinge of jealousy and disappointment starting to come on, I took a breath and decided to practice appreciative joy for him in that very same moment. Mudita was becoming more and more my default practice in these types of situations, and what a good way to further prepare for my talk. I closed my eyes in the middle of the loud sounds of conversation, tea and coffee cups clinking, and the background buzz of a New York City coffee shop. As I sat there finding my way to feeling happiness and joy for this total stranger, all of a sudden I felt a soft tap on my right shoulder. I slowly opened my eyes and turned my head to find that it was him! After a moment, he smiled and said, "Hi, I noticed you seem to have quite a bit of papers with you and I just wanted to know if you'd like to trade seats with me, so you could have more room for your things." I instantly smiled. If I had any remaining doubt about the effectiveness of the heart practices, in that moment it was gone. My heart felt even happier and brighter. "Wow, that was fast. Mudita really works," I thought to myself, before replying, "Why, yes, thank you." And he walked me over to the table, picked up his notebook, and wished me a good day, returning to the seat at the community table I had just come from.

Sometimes we can feel really alone and not a part of the world even in the middle of a densely populated metropolitan area like New York City. Yet sharing in another's suffering as well as in their joy and happiness immediately makes us feel connected, even with a total stranger. The power of mudita can be encompassed in one simple phrase: your happiness makes me happy. Tried and true, I have put this statement to the test over the years. To feel happy for lovers walking hand in hand down the street, to delight in the radiating laughter of a small child running carefreely in the city park's playground, to notice good friendship between two people reveling in each other's company at lunch together, to let the simple smile of someone walking by us as they chat away on the phone be a source of joy for us too—this sharing and taking part in the daily ordinary moments of the happiness we see around us affirms our place in the human experience. It's the basic recognition that just as we breathe, we also have the basic capacity for joy. Taking pleasure in others' joy opens up the wellspring of our innate right to turn toward joy and experience it ourselves. Appreciative joy lets us see our happiness is others' happiness, and theirs is ours.

In today's meditation, you'll work with some beautiful phrases for rejoicing in others' joy, gladness, and good fortune. You'll be calling to mind someone in your life you can more easily feel happy for. Let these mudita mantras sink into your mind and heart, and notice the instant effects, just as I did in the middle of New York City.

---

today's meditation

FINDING YOUR JOY IN THE JOY OF OTHERS

- Sit comfortably in your meditation space.
- Let your body find ease and a sweet familiarity of arriving home to your practice today.
- When you're ready, softly close your eyes.
- Guide your attention to your heart space. Rest in the rhythms of the breath here as the breath moves your body.
- Begin to call to mind someone for whom it is easy for you to feel rejoicing energy for. This can be a person you know really well and whom you enjoy seeing happy and successful.
- Take a moment to think about a recent time they were the recipient of good fortune or felt happy. Reflect on the causes and conditions that lead them to experiencing this joy and happiness.
- And with them in mind, silently recite the following mudita mantras in your mind.

mudita mantras

May your happiness and good fortune grow and increase.
May your happiness never diminish or leave you.
Your happiness makes me happy.
Thank you for sharing your happiness with me.

- Keep repeating these mudita mantras as you rejoice and delight in their happiness.
- Discover the resonance of their joy in your own heart.
- Continue this practice for the remaining time in your meditation.
- When you are ready, slowly open your eyes.

PRACTICE NOTE: If you found it difficult to feel joy for someone, know that is perfectly okay. Mudita is not something we are used to doing in modern Western culture! If this is the case for you, my suggestion is to see if there's anything you feel grateful for that they have done or to generate loving-kindness or compassion for them if they've recently gone through a difficult time. Remember, the essence of mudita is to sympathize with others' experiences of the heart. Take your time and find your doorway into feeling genuine joy.

For your practice reflection today, journal what it feels like to experience appreciative joy for someone in your body, heart, and mind. Allow your mindful awareness to guide you during your heart writing. Many people experience mudita as a warm, open expansiveness in their chest and heart space or a lightening and uplifting of their actual heart. You may notice a smile is more of a regular occurrence since you started your joy practice or your mind feels less bogged down and freer. Now, move right into the following reflections.

REFLECTION QUESTION 1: How does rejoicing for others feel in my body, heart, and mind?

REFLECTION QUESTION 2: What have I noticed so far this week when practicing mudita? (Replace with metta or karuna if needed.)

Once you've answered today's questions in your practice journal, place your hand over your heart, close your eyes, and thank your mind and heart for expanding your wellspring of joy as you support the amplification of joy and happiness within others' hearts as well.

TODAY'S MUDITA MOMENT

Today's daily practice is going to be taking your appreciative joy on the road. Whenever you witness someone else's joy or happiness as you move throughout your day, send them one of the mudita mantras from today's meditation. (Of course, you can do this silently in your mind. They don't need to know you're practicing mudita for them! Unless you feel inspired to tell them.) Then take a moment and savor the goodness and happiness in your own heart after you've wished their happiness and joy to never diminish and to only grow and increase.

———

DAY 20

a love language

The flowering of love is meditation.
—*J. Krishnamurti*

RECENTLY I WAS ASKED in a podcast interview what meditation meant to me in one word. Here was my response: "Love."[23] Meditation is learning how to love properly. In fact, I know of no other training that points you back to the true nature of love over and over again like the practice of meditation. No matter what our experience is or what technique we employ, whether we even intend to or not, eventually we all bump into love. Just like thoughts are inevitable during meditation, learning what love is, is inevitable too.

Mudita will stretch us. It will ask us to choose love over and over again. In meditation, we are learning to rest our own hearts and minds in the present moment, with a sense of safety and in the name of nonharm. We are creating a foundation within ourselves built on our own understanding and uncovering of love's ways. Love is what we touch down upon when the heart and the mind are in their natural resting states. Love is what we build our inner home out of when we are practicing with the brahma-viharas.

Appreciative joy is the intentional offering of this inner love we've accumulated from treading in love's waters over the years. Metta, karuna, and mudita weather us like a river's currents smooth out the rough edges of a stone—the more exposure it has to the river's timeless ebbs and flows, the smoother it gets. Traditionally, this sharing of the heart is a practice of generosity. Love and wisdom are meant to be shared. The human heart is designed to give and to take just by how it functions within the ecosystem of the body. Our happiness, joy, compassion, kindness, and equanimity are the ways in which our practice is communicated to the world through these natural laws of input and output. Desmond Tutu, archbishop emeritus of South Africa, phrases the generosity of the heart and our joy in this way: "It is in giving that we receive." The less self-centering we are in our spiritual pursuits, he goes on to say, the more "we grow in self-forgetfulness—in a remarkable way I mean we discover that we are filled with joy."[24]

generosity is love

I invite you to pause for a moment and take in the archbishop's words: "It is in giving that we receive." Notice how your heart may respond to this call for generosity. Joy and happiness are the language of love, just like compassion and kindness are. When sharing in another's happiness by practicing appreciative joy, we are communicating to the recipients of our rejoicing that we stand for love. When we let our joyfulness become an expression of love's boundless ability to overcome grief, loss, small-mindedness, jealousy, or any urges to smother someone else's success, or even someone else's love story, each ordinary moment of the day takes on the potential to become extraordinary.

Earlier in our list of the multiple expressions of joy, I shared about the flavor of joy called "elevation," the warm and uplifting feeling we experience when we see unexpected acts of kindness and human goodness. As we practice being generous in our language of love, we look for these snapshots of elevation in our own heart and within the delighted faces of others. When we approach sharing our loving heart in this way, we can watch our own joy and the happiness of others bloom. Joy is expansive, and giving supports our heart's expanse. The essential question becomes, can we be brave and confident and free enough to give our love away like an undammed river? Can we relinquish it, spread it, and let our shared joy flood across the earth in the most extraordinary daily and ordinary of ways?

---

today's meditation

GIVE A FLOWER OF GENEROSITY, GET A FLOWER OF JOY

In this mudita meditation I will guide you through a visualization, inviting you to offer a flower of generosity to someone and then receive a flower of joy in return. The flower you give can symbolize any of love's faces. For instance, if you feel inspired to share the feeling of love that is present in your practice—or the flower of happiness, appreciative joy, or compassion—then this can be the flower you give. The flower you receive can be representational of any joy you become aware of during the act of giving or the gratitude from someone else for you sharing your generous heart.

Let's get settled in to begin.

- Find your way to a comfortable posture as you invite in a deep, settling breath.
- Close your eyes.

- Spend a few moments resting your attention in your body.
- Guide your attention to the area of your heart.
- Gently rest your awareness here, noticing the natural pulsations of your heart.
- Connect to any feelings of warmth, love, or nurturance that may be present while allowing whatever is here to be here with great tenderness and care.
- With your awareness centered in your heart, start to visualize someone whom you'd like to share your practice with today. This can be someone you know well or barely at all. Just someone who feels right to give and receive with.
- Imagine that they are right before you and send some good wishes their way. It can be the mudita mantra of "May your joy and happiness grow and increase today" or a more general sentiment of wishing them to feel good or well.
- Then imagine your heartfelt wishes become a beautiful flower being held in your hand. You may see the luminous petals sparkling and notice the deep-green stem gently held between your fingers and thumb.
- This flower holds any part of your practice that you want to give today. Whether it is love, loving-kindness, attention, support, or joy.
- Now extend this flower of generosity to them. Notice their response and their heart's delight.
- After they receive your flower, imagine them taking a flower of joy from their heart and offering it right back to you.
- As you receive this flower of their generosity in your hand now, feel your heart amplify with their joy.
- Keep giving and receiving a flower of generosity and a flower of joy with them for as long as you would like to.
- When you are ready to end your meditation, spend a moment resting the palms of your hands over your heart.

- Take one more full breath in and out and slowly open your eyes.

Take out your practice journal and let the words start to flow! Write any experiences or insight that came up from your meditation. How did sharing your practice feel to you? When ready, take today's journaling practice a step further by answering the following reflection question.

REFLECTION QUESTION: To whom and where can I extend my generosity of joy?

TODAY'S MUDITA MOMENT

Generosity expands the state of your heart. It becomes a way to share your practice with others. In meditation you train your heart's ability to generously share itself unbounded and unafraid. In doing this, you create a womb of love in which others feel as though they can take refuge and rest in. This is why mudita is so medicinal—it holds the great healing power of love.

Today, notice any natural inclination you have to share love or joy. This can be by smiling at a stranger, opening the door for someone, or saying thank you to someone who shows kindness to you. Appreciative joy is a great connector. It helps us feel a part of the world, like we belong to the pulse of humanity. Give generosity at any chance you get and then notice the joy that follows closely on the heels of your sharing.

———

DAY 21

———

true celebration

Give the world your love, your service,
your healing, but you can also give it
your joy. This, too, is a great gift.
—*Archbishop Emeritus Desmond Tutu*

WELCOME TO THE END of Week 3! Reading these words and getting excited for your practice today is cause enough to celebrate! Let's take a moment to honor the great work you've done. As you've learned, feeling and sharing joy is no small thing. Joy can be felt far and wide. It can turn someone's day right around the moment they encounter *your* ability to rejoice. Today we celebrate your practice and newfound superhuman power of joy by focusing on a few facets of joy that are rather lively and ecstatic. In true celebratory fashion, let's dive into the pure rapture and bliss of altruism and take on the natural high of celebrating others' success, prosperity, and well-being alongside our own.

altruistic love and joy

Altruism is the selfless concern for the well-being of others. The Buddhist view has a way of defining it as altruistic love:

"the wish that all beings may find happiness and the causes of happiness."[25] This precise aspiration is the ripe training ground for true rapture and joy. So often rapture and bliss are siloed away as an individual experience and are interpreted through our own pleasure. Breaking open our joy paradigm is part of letting joy take on its full expression.

Have you ever felt your heart explode with happiness on someone else's behalf? Perhaps your friend shares news that her lover asked for her hand in marriage, or you hear from a fellow meditator that they feel connected to their expansive, loving, boundless, authentic buddha nature for the first time in their adult life. Or feeling the active pleasure of being lost in sweet commune with nature as you walk in a park and experience enough selflessness to let your heart open to feeling happy *with* the world. This kind of happiness and bliss is directly connected to being in relationship with another person or with the world around you. Altruistic joy is recognizing this interconnectedness and feeling unbounded enough to take on others' happiness as your own.

be joy positive

Fellow Buddhist teacher Heather Prete, my colleague and dear friend, teaches the heart practices in a real celebratory way. When introducing metta and mudita practice, with arms stretched wide and in total exuberance, she tells her students to use the following phrases as they practice wishing others loving-kindness and sympathetic joy: "Yay for you! Yay for me! And yay for us!" This yay-like mentality is the very key to feeling the pleasure point of life's good moments as well as a real acknowledgment of how precious happiness is. Letting the heart dwell in the healing and relief of true happiness gives an inner taste of freedom beyond grasping or feeling scared this happiness won't last. We hold our own happiness and the happiness of others with an open-palmed hand, elated in its presence and feeling the deep-seated contentment and strength of celebrating it in this moment while knowing at some point it will change, reconfigure, and transform. Being joy positive is like highlighting and holding happiness when it is here, so it can be appreciated and fully valued. Celebrating joy is a very respectful practice. It respects the humanness of our happiness and those times we gather together to celebrate one another.

Our benevolence blossoms in the opportunities to commemorate one another's highs as well as being able to hold one another's lows. Joy and compassion are inextricably linked and interwoven in the heart. A number of times when I'm working with a student one-on-one on their meditation practice and after hearing a story of their difficult meditation session or all of the thoughts they've been having, my response is, "Good, I'm happy for you." A little bewildered, they ask, "But why?" My response: "These times of turbulence will give you more perspective on the equanimity and pleasure that will inevitably visit you too." Turning toward the opportunity to really immerse ourselves in the good when it's here gives us the balance to keep meeting life's next moments.

Mudita is our reminder to dance freely when we're given the opportunity, to let go in the ecstasy of joy's bliss and life's happy tears; to be moved by witnessing others' pleasure or the miracle of love between two people; to know the more we celebrate each other finding happiness and the causes of happiness, the more we all grow our adoration of life's boundless beauty and limitless wonder. Mudita frees us to feel the fullness of our existence and to let in happiness without hesitation.

In today's practice I will guide you in feeling the rapture and delight of celebrating someone's happiness while noticing your own heart's joy.

When you are ready, let's celebrate and begin!

today's meditation

CELEBRATION MEDITATION

- Relax your body into your meditation space.
- When you're ready, gently close your eyes and take a few breaths to signal the start of your meditation.
- Bring to mind someone you'd like to celebrate. Remember that this is a heart celebration, so you'll be opening your heart to feeling the contact high of delight from their happiness and success. Maybe this is a good friend who has just gained some monumental success or a person you don't know well whose prosperity has inspired you in some way.
- Rest in the field of rejoice for this person's happiness. Contemplate how precious their happiness is and take joy in all the causes of their happiness.
- If you'd like, you can send them the following mudita mantras.

mudita mantras for celebration

May you continue to find happiness and the causes
* of happiness.*
May you find true freedom and joy in all of your
* success.*
I celebrate your happiness today. I celebrate your joy.

- Take notice of your own heart space right now. Are there any feelings of delight, rapture, or celebration present?
- Is your heart dancing or fluttering? Feeling light or boundless? It's okay if this isn't the case. Simply notice where you are on the joy index.
- When you're ready, invite in a long, slow, steady breath and release this breath as you open your eyes.
- Stretch your body in any way that it would like. If it feels good to you, lift your arms up high and feel the rapture and delight from celebrating joy today.

True celebration is the essence of rejoicing. It is the uplift we all live for and adds endless meaning and fond memories to our lives. Pause for a moment, pick up your practice journal, and spend a few minutes reflecting on the following writing prompt before you start the rest of your day.

REFLECTION QUESTION: How can I support and celebrate others' success and happiness in my life?

Let the words flow. After your journaling, make sure to recap and reflect upon the big week you just completed exploring the practice ground of a joyful mind and heart! Enjoy this moment of reflection. Celebrate all of the inner work you accomplished over the past seven days and the seeds of genuine happiness you have planted far and wide.

TODAY'S MUDITA MOMENT

You are responsible for your own happiness. You can still be in touch with happiness and joy even in the midst of hardship or stress. Rejoicing in other people's happiness amplifies joy and abundance in your life. To end the week of mudita practice, look for all of the ways you can celebrate joy and happiness today. Be a joy promoter and a joy enthusiast. Take any opportunity to recognize others' good ideas, achievements, good news, and success and watch how your own heart feels fuller, happier, and more content.

––––––

TEACHINGS ON EQUANIMITY

Upekkha (equanimity) is the expression of our innermost freedom and liberation. It is both the sweet relief of truly feeling at ease in the world and the natural resting ground of the heart. Upekkha, the fourth and final heart quality, is the hearth of the brahma-viharas. Without it the other heart qualities of loving-kindness, compassion, and appreciative joy may ask too much of us at times before we are ready. For me, without upekkha balancing the pendulum swings of my heart and mind, I can easily experience compassion fatigue, empathy burnout, and feel underresourced to be in my full expression of kindness and joy. I so need to have my feet anchored and tethered to the earth as I walk the path of the heart, as it makes the lifelong journey a sustainable one.

Where the other three brahma-viharas may impassion us, propelling us forward with the fire of a compassionate response and calls for kindness and the extreme highs of joy and celebration, upekkha is like the yin to the other brahma-viharas yang. It is the cooling agent of the heart, landing us right in the middle of mindfulness and the heart qualities. In many ways, equanimity is the heart's iteration of mindful awareness. It gives us the poise to be able to sustain practicing the brahma-viharas in the long run. Are you ready and excited for this last week of practice? I hope so. It is the final building block of making your heart an unshakable home within!

understanding equanimity

Upekkha, translated from Pali as "balance," centers us in the reality of things exactly as they are. It gives us the skillful means to see our own hearts and minds clearly so we can ultimately be in authentic alignment with exactly where we are internally. The Sanskrit word for the fourth abode of the heart, *upeksha*, is translated as "equanimity," which is often described as an inner state of evenness—an evenness of mind and heart in the midst of life's endless ups and downs, pulling toward and pushing away, liking and disliking, wanting and wishing away.

As you'll learn further this week, life is an endless stream of pleasant or unpleasant impressions, or sometimes neither. How can we be with this? How do we handle the ever-changing landscape of our present moments? Equanimity becomes our how. It is indeed the way we catch ourselves before we spin out into any extreme reactions or mindsets. It is the middle path between getting overwhelmed, falling into well-worn habit grooves in the mind, or becoming hypervigilant with our conditioned way of trying to stop or control life's changing currents.

I like to think of equanimity as holding a balanced view or choosing a balanced perspective and remaining balanced in the *middle of it all*—not too reactionary or defensive, and not too apathetic, checked out, or sullen. Equanimity yields the ability to find wise relationships to our changing experiences. It's a balancing rudder so we don't tip our boats too far this way or that way, so that we find just the right balance to be with the changing currents of reality. Evenness of mind and heart allow us to understand, see, and accept things as they are. More so, this home of inner equilibrium gives us the wisdom to know when to let go.

EQUANIMITY IS A FEELING YOU FEEL

What I love most about equanimity is it's a quality and state to be experienced and felt. Many of my students share how equanimity is their first sign that meditation is working for them. I often hear, "I just feel more centered and more at ease within myself," or "I just *feel* more peaceful, I can't really explain it." For me too, equanimity is often what I feel first—an emanating state of grace from my heart, or more so the direct channel between my awareness and my heart. It's a feeling where I know, without logic or reason, my chitta is turned on. How this inner light of heart awareness gets flipped on is through my daily practice. Within the first few minutes of my meditations I feel my heart and mind touch and form their connection for the day. All of a sudden, an undisputable sense of inner centeredness and peace arises, and each time I know it the split second it happens. Equanimity may just be the reason I have come back to daily meditation for over a decade. And it has most definitely been a palpable signpost that meditation is working.

how to practice

Much like with each of the heart's abodes, the way to approach growing our equanimity is by diving right into it, fearlessly and, if ready, with abandon. Naturally, within equanimity lies an immeasurable amount of confidence and trust in the act of dwelling directly within our lives. Magically, you have already been practicing with equanimity in these past twenty-one days and for the entire life span of your meditation practice. You first learn the quality of equanimity in your basic mindfulness sitting practice. Meditation *is* a practice of equanimity. This is why we start each of our days with the same reliable sequence of instructions: make home in your body, find traction and steadiness with the breath, rest in this moment. As imprints and snapshots of the past or future come and go, as our emotional lives reveal themselves, we sit with the feelings and let the thoughts go, recentering ourselves in the great equanimity of the present moment.

Here are the glowing faces of equanimity and some ways we will be working with upekkha during our week together. Equanimity means:

Letting go
Nonjudgment
Nonattachment
Meeting the moment as it is
Mindfully responding with kindness, compassion,
    and joy (applying the other heart qualities)

You may notice that these flavors of equanimity are wise means of working with the inevitable energies we encounter in the world. Equanimity is most synonymous with wisdom when we are working with equanimity in an intentional way. Our grounded hearts, our vows of mindfulness and compassion, our promises of nonharm *are* our lived intentions. The way we are able to practice these aspirations of the heart is by finding our footing in the even playing field of equanimity—free from being bound or tied by our passions or aggressions, our desires or delusion, our preferences and opinions.

Over the next week you will learn how equanimity is one of the biggest contributing factors to living a meaningful life and feeling fulfilled, peaceful, and content no matter what circumstances you may find yourself in. Each day is full of rich principles and practices, tying all four heart qualities together through the manifestation of upekkha.

- On Day 22 you'll learn more about the true nature of equanimity and begin to work with feeling tones and nonjudgmental awareness (one of my most favorite equanimity practices).
- During Days 23 and 24, you'll go through the deep meaningful inner work of acceptance and real resilience.
- Day 25 will teach you how to access inner stillness at any time.
- Then you'll meditate on the nature of reality on Day 26 (no biggie, right?) and connect to a fundamental state of okayness that is always there for you within the direct experience of the present moment.
- To celebrate the end of your twenty-eight days of heart training, on Days 27 and 28 you'll strengthen your sense of inner freedom and learn how to move forward living openheartedly.

I'm so happy that you are here and have arrived at this life changing week of practice together. Let's begin.

DAY 22

———

finding evenness within

We already have everything we need.
—*Pema Chödrön*

BEING A LONGTIME MEDITATOR, I had always prided myself on having a level of perceived centeredness and confidence. After all, feeling more self-assured had been one of the very first tangible effects I had experienced from meditation. I'll never forget that early morning I had my own cliché movie moment a few feet between my front door and my car as I was on my way to work. All of a sudden I was stopped in my tracks by what felt like a force beyond myself, but also from a feeling deep within my own being. The weight of my work bags made my shoulders surrender toward the ground as all of the rushing forward momentum halted and I closed my eyes. Feeling the cool morning air against my cheeks, I realized I felt more centered and whole than I had felt in a really long time. My awareness rested in my heart space, and there was a happy confidence alive and emanating from within me. I felt more like my authentic self in that moment than perhaps since my young childhood days. I recalled how lately I hadn't been as wishy-washy with my opinions quite as much. Over the past

195

couple of weeks I had spoken up more at team meetings, and the constant self–second guessing about every single decision and choice in front of me had almost vanished.

Before leaving for work that day, I had just finished my morning meditation practice. "The practice is *really* working," I thought. Then the words "So, this is what it feels like to be at home within yourself?" floated across my heart and mind. This pivotal moment in my life was one of the main reasons I felt inspired to keep meditating every day over the years. Life was different. I was different, yet at the same time more me. It was like a great returning home to who I really was and a realigning with my buddha nature.

Ever since that ordinary morning took on a tone of extraordinary centeredness, I have really valued my found sense of inner stability. Yet as I walked through the main meditation hall on day one of my first weeklong silent meditation retreat, I couldn't help but notice certain individuals had such a grounding energy to them! One man in particular, who I had been meditating close to that morning, expressed such dignity in his meditation posture—never flinching or moving. He was like a magnificent mountain of meditation groundedness, solidness, serenity, safety, and calm. I felt so at ease just being near him. As the week unfolded, there were a few others I earmarked in my awareness who exuded the same qualities as he did. I always made sure I was practicing my walking meditation close to one of them, and I continued to sit near the man who embodied such deep practice throughout the whole week.

Days after the retreat ended, I was back in Los Angeles at my daily tea shop and I ran into a close friend who I practiced meditation with regularly. I told her I had just come back from my first weeklong retreat in total silence and practice. She was looking at me rather intently, almost like she was seeing through me or was attuning to something around me or beyond me. After a moment she gently offered, "Amanda, you seem so much more solid." A smile crossed my face as well as my heart. "I am," I responded. "I am." Though I did feel more solid in myself, in further reflection months later I admitted to myself that I had a pattern of finding my sense of center in others, particularly my boyfriends and romantic partners. I was used to giving my center away and finding it in them, rather than within myself. This had been illuminated by my relying on the other experienced meditators around me to make a connection with the depths of my own inner stability and equanimity. Since the retreat, I had been feeling not as centered and solid in myself, and I could see that I was searching for solidness outside of myself again. With this uncovering years after my equanimity movie moment midwalk to work, I knew I had more work to do to find my authentic sense of inner solidness. So I remembered a teaching that is supposed to help you remain steady in the flux of daily feelings and experiences. And it instantly helped me start to build my own sustainable solid core and center. I'm so excited to share this very same practice with you today!

your key to deciphering reality

To start the week of growing your own home base within your heart and mind, I'm going to share with you an awesome meditation technique that is key to unlocking your sense of steadfastness and unshakable inner stability. The technique deciphers our present-moment experiences; it's a way for us to wisely relate to anything comprising any present moment that we are in. The Buddha taught that every single moment contains the feeling tone of the following three categories of experience: pleasant, unpleasant, or neutral. Traditionally known as *vedana*, or the registering of the three qualities of feelings found in any experience. The practice is to be mindful of which one you are in.

Vedana is the feeling and the knowing of the feeling tone of each present moment. This is an incredibly helpful practice to both gain insight and maintain your balance in any given situation. For instance, let's say you are about to step into a meeting with your supervisor at work and they haven't told you why they want to meet with you. Going in you can say to yourself, "Well, this will either go one of three ways. It will be pleasant, unpleasant, or neutral (neither pleasant nor unpleasant)." If in the meeting you receive praise or good news, you can label the experience as "pleasant" and respond accordingly by enjoying and appreciating the pleasant feeling. If you find yourself fielding some feedback or you hear some not-so-great news, you can acknowledge the meeting is now "unpleasant" and have compassion for yourself and your colleagues. If the meeting turns into more of a check-in—just a quick catch up on your projects with no big updates either way—you can label it "neutral" and simply allow the conversation to unfold.

As you'll learn more on Day 27, usually with pleasant feelings we tend to grasp tightly and do everything in our power to never let the good feelings end, such as becoming attached to hearing praise and validation from others at work. With unpleasant experiences, normally we want to exit the situation as soon as possible and distract ourselves with the quickest hit of pleasantness we can find with food, flirtation, or diving into our phone.

Today you are going to get down the fundamental noting of the three feeling tones of experience so you can start to see how this nonjudgmental perspective helps you keep or regain your equanimity. This type of awareness is a real step toward feeling the real freedom of taking ownership over your perceptions and ability to find your way back to center and create a steady evenness within.

PRACTICE NOTE: A common question I get asked is "Isn't labeling our experiences as pleasant, unpleasant, or neutral a judgment?" The good news is it is different. Deciphering our reality is not a judgment nor is it an analytical thought in the mind. Noting the *vedana*, or the underlining feeling tone, is recognizing experience for what it is, simply being with that and stopping there. We drop the stories, opinions, and judgments, which lead us a step closer to true nonjudgmental awareness and learning how to be with each present moment exactly as it is.

---

today's meditation

NONJUDGMENTAL AWARENESS MEDITATION

- Allow yourself to become settled and comfortable in your meditation space.
- Take a deep breath and then rest your attention in your lower body for the next few minutes. Feel your own mountainlike qualities within, the support of the seat or surface beneath you, and the strength of your bones holding your body in its meditation position.
- Notice how you too can be like a mountain. Finding steadiness and evenness within regardless of any thoughts, feelings, or sensations you may become aware of.
- With a kind and warm focus, place your attention on the breath and see if you can sense that same sort of steadiness and constant fortitude within the breath, letting the breath come and go with a natural grace and ease.

- Now, whenever you become aware of something other than the breath—a passing thought in the mind, a memory, an inclination to think about anything happening later in your day, or a feeling associated with these thoughts and their corresponding sensations in the body—I want you to note whether the feeling of the moment is:

Pleasant
Unpleasant
Neutral

- Then with a nonjudgmental ease, guide your attention back to the breath.
- Your practice will consist of these three notes—pleasant, unpleasant, or neutral—silently in the mind and the familiarity of returning to your home base within the breath.
- Continue this for the rest of your meditation practice time.
- When bringing your practice to a close, let any noting in the mind pause for just a moment. Recenter yourself in the sensation of just the breath.
- Feel any qualities of evenness, balance, stability, or peace.
- Then open your eyes.

Balance is found by noting the vedana of any experience. The moment you attune to the pleasantness, unpleasantness, or neutrality of any situation is the same moment you release yourself from being caught up in the highs or lows, wanting or not wanting, liking or wishing away.

Take out your practice journal now and spend a few minutes reflecting on the following journal questions.

REFLECTION QUESTION 1: What does balance mean to me?

REFLECTION QUESTION 2: Where in my life can I use more balance and less judgment?

When you're finished writing, pause for a moment and sense into the evenness and balance within your own heart, body, and mind. Take a deep breath and start your day from this feeling of centeredness and self-connection.

EQUANIMITY IN ACTION

One of my most trusted and reliable daily practice tools is noting experiences as pleasant, unpleasant, or neutral. I've spent weeks practicing this, just strolling through one moment to the next with the knowing awareness of which feeling tone is at play. For example, when I encounter traffic in Los Angeles, San Francisco, or New York City, I'll start noting over and over again, "Ah this is unpleasant. Unpleasant . . . unpleasant . . . unpleasant!" Then when I arrive at my destination, I note, "Ah, now this is pleasant."

All within a matter of minutes and hours we can experience all three categories of feeling tones millions of times throughout each day. Equanimity and emotional freedom lie within this simple tool of noting your experience. So today, get psyched and have fun noting your present moments as pleasant, unpleasant, or neutral.

DAY 23

---

acceptance

If you let go a little, you will have a little peace.
If you let go a lot, you will have a lot of peace.
—Ajahn Chah

TODAY YOU ARE GOING to arrive in the realm of true acceptance, a vital ingredient in cultivating equanimity and the miraculous path to feeling fulfilled, peaceful, and at ease no matter what circumstances you may find yourself in. The Tibetan word for equanimity is *tang-nyom. Tang* means "to release or let go," and *nyom* means "to equalize." This translation of equanimity points us to an important truth: we regain our sense of center and inner balance by deciding to release and let go. What exactly are we letting go of, you may ask? Our habitual human tendency of so dearly wanting to control our lives and reality. I'm sure we can all find some identification with this concept in our own way almost instantaneously.

As you learned yesterday, the ability to identify the underlying feeling tone of any given moment is a real step to mental and emotional freedom. This is mindfulness at its finest! Through learning to recognize your reality, you take the first step toward accepting your reality. Rather than trying to manipulate and control your life for higher degrees of pleasantness and less pain, you move into a state of being *with* the world. You step into the truth of the moment, exactly as it is. The heart knows this dance with the universe so well. The minute you accept and let go of needing to control situations or other people, you will start to feel the ease of equanimity and the reestablishment of your inner stability.

authentic acceptance

During today's practice it can be helpful to keep in the back of your mind the following natural sequence for authentic acceptance. Each step leads to the next as you genuinely surrender into what each present moment holds.

> Cultivate Nonjudgment (being in a right relationship
> with the present moment) ⟶
> Noncontrol (acceptance) ⟶ Letting Go (freedom)

Really, when we practice this progression we're pointing ourselves to the ripe potential of acceptance as we move from living our lives solely from the mind to becoming more heart-based. The mind loves to create a mental map of how it thinks our lives should go—a mental fixation of having one goal, for example, and only one road leading to this one goal. Have you ever found yourself thinking, "All I want is my epic dream house. It has to have five bedrooms, two fireplaces, and a backyard." Or "My perfect partner will be six feet two, have brown hair, brown eyes, be kind yet successful, and oh, they have to make more money than me." These desires are very specific versions of happiness and fulfillment leaving only one avenue to arrive there.

When you are living with a controlling, forcing frequency and not yet working in alignment with the balancing energy of acceptance, your dreams, goals, and desires can only look one way, according to your one vision and your one tiny idea of it. You are probably getting the idea of just how constricting and limiting this way of being is. It leaves little room for spontaneity or the space to let things just be and breathe for a moment, let alone updating your aspirations according to what *is* actually happening or what it is you actually want and are in most alignment with now.

I will never forget reading *When Things Fall Apart* by Pema Chödrön. Luckily for me, it graced my bedside nightstand for the chapters of my life when I needed these words of wisdom on how to let go of the need to control and fixate on only one version of my desired reality the most. She ends the epic road map of how to navigate our most heartbreaking moments in life—the kind where our dreams, fantasies, and expectations we are holding all combust, fall apart, and no longer align with what is actually occurring in our life story. She writes,

> The path is not Route 66—destination, Los Angeles. It's not as if we can take out a map and figure that this year we might make it to Gallup, New Mexico, and maybe by 2001, we'll be in L.A. The path is uncharted. It comes into existence moment by moment and at the same time drops away behind us. It's like riding a train sitting backwards. We can't see where we're headed, only where we've been.[26]

The last time I read these words at the end of *When Things Fall Apart*, I was at the end of my own nomadic journey of eighteen months. Admittedly I had a deep desire and intention to land back in LA full time. Yet, if anything, those eighteen months of being unrooted and untethered to a physical location and home had brought me to fully stepping into my true mobile home within. I had always talked about and taught "no matter where you are, you are home." Those months of travel made me embody and understand this truth without a shadow of a doubt in my heart. I had also come to understand, to really live this and breathe this: you have to let go. And when I finally—completely with every ounce of my authentic being—let go of Route 66, destination, Los Angeles, the universe came in and gave me the very obvious signs. I knew it was time to head back and find an external home on the beach and in the mountains of LA.

Equanimity will always align you back into authenticity. And it will help you form a deep trust with the natural rhythms of life itself, where the ego's mad small ideas loosen their grip. Peace is at your fingertips. Your mind and heart find contentment even mid-unraveling of your dreams and goals. Acceptance becomes your wise form of truly letting go back into equanimity over and over again.

In today's meditation I will share with you a few of my most cherished mantras for acceptance and releasing the need to control. May they serve you deeply in letting go of your destinations, just long enough for life to come in and walk with you as your next present moments unfold.

---

today's meditation

LETTING GO OF THE NEED TO CONTROL

- Take a moment to settle into your meditation space.
- Invite a few cleansing breaths into your body. When you are ready, gently close your eyes.
- Spend the next few minutes establishing your awareness in your body.
- Let your attention touch down into your body resting upon the earth below it. If you'd like, you can even place your

fingertips and palms of your hands on the ground beside you, sensing into the unwavering support of the earth body beneath you and all around you.

- Recenter yourself in a comfortable position for your meditation.
- Watch your body breathe with your awareness for the next few minutes, gaining clarity with the breath, finding equilibrium and equanimity within the breath, and letting go of any thoughts in the mind.
- Meditation is a natural releasing and letting go, and then choosing to begin again.
- As you continue to rest your attention within your body breathing, I invite you to begin the silent repetition of the following mantras of acceptance and letting go in the mind.

mantras for acceptance and release

May I accept this moment exactly as it is.
May I accept myself exactly as I am.
May I learn to let go. May I learn to let go.
I am listening. Tell me what to do, what to say,
and where to go.

- Repeat these phrases in the mind for the remainder of your meditation.
- Let both the mantras and the breath lead the way into the middle of this present moment exactly as it is.
- To bring your meditation to a close today, place the palms of your hands over your heart for a moment and feel the warmth of acceptance and the healing energy of letting go.
- Touch your fingers back down to the earth.
- When you are ready, gently open your eyes.

This meditation may leave you feeling raw, cracked open, exhilarated, or vulnerable. Remember to extend acceptance to even the fruits of your meditation practice!

Right now or before bed tonight, spend some quality time with your practice journal on the following contemplation.

REFLECTION QUESTION: Where can I move into acceptance and give up my need to control the outcome?

I encourage you to let this be a longer writing session today and to be compassionately honest with yourself as you move through this healing process of releasing the suffering that comes when we try so hard to control and manipulate our world. Make sure to also practice joy for yourself when you're done writing. This is no small practice to take on. Cultivating equanimity can be actually quite joyous and feel so beautifully good!

EQUANIMITY IN ACTION

Today's equanimity practice is to continue your sequential authentic acceptance practice of:

1. NONJUDGMENT—you can continue to note pleasant, unpleasant, neutral if you'd like.
2. NONCONTROL OR ACCEPTANCE—repeat any of today's acceptance mantras on the spot to help you arrive to a space of acceptance.
3. LET GO—feel the felt sense of letting go and the rebalancing into equanimity the moment you choose to let go.

Enjoy the freedom this three-step practice brings!

———

DAY 24

---

real resilience

*Struggle can be our greatest call to courage
and the clearest path to a wholehearted life.*
—Brené Brown

TERESA, A LONGTIME STUDENT of mine, has been through a lot in a human lifetime—from a traumatic childhood, to several relationships with men who had little to no respect for her, to having a daughter born with autism as a single mom. When we met, she was at her very last straw. She started our first session with, "I just don't know how I can keep going anymore. The only reason why I get up every day is because of Lily." Lily is her daughter. "If Lily wasn't fully dependent on me as she most likely will be for her entire life, I really think I would . . . well, I'm not sure what I would do."

I've come to learn just how so many of my students drawn to my classes arrive at meditation's doorstep because of brokenness. As one of my meditation mentors, Matthew Brensilver, often says when he is teaching, "We don't come to meditation because things are going well in our lives." As much as I raised my eyebrows the first few times I heard this, I couldn't help but recognize the genuine truth embedded in this statement.

In many ways this was my truth. What really brought me to a daily meditation practice was being on my knees, looking at the broken pieces of my life, with the genuine need for healing. I see a version of this story in so many meditators. Deep down we know we need a path to understand what has transpired in our lives thus far and how to work with the remnants. Somewhere within us is a call for healing; somehow we know resilience, growth, and understanding are out there.

A few months after Teresa started her daily meditation practice, she came to one of our weekly sessions with an update: "You know, Amanda, I don't feel quite as weighted down by everything that has happened or even by what is happening now. I still freak out. I still lose my patience with my daughter. But something really interesting has begun to happen where I feel like I recover quicker. I feel like I find my way back to my inner kindness and can rest in the pause before my reaction a bit more. This has made me feel like a stronger person as of late. I don't feel so decimated by life anymore." Teresa had found the soft spot within her pain and suffering. She had found the through line of inner strength that moves us from brokenness to resilience.

recovery by way of resilience

Resilience can be defined as our capacity to recover from our difficulties and what life throws our way. Through the natural cultivation of upekkha that happens when we commit to a regular meditation practice, I have come to add on to this definition. Resilience is our ability to recover from our hardships and setbacks and to find our way back to our built-in baseline of equanimity. It is our ability to recover back to centeredness, to come back home. This work is by no means easy. Real resilience requires the strength and courage to see ourselves and our lives clearly. We see where we are still hurt, fearful, and running at half steam, and how we're trying to learn how to fly again though our setbacks have clipped our wings.

Perceiving our lives clearly and with mindfulness makes room for a powerful shift to occur. Within the soft spots of our brokenness lies the potential for a new way of relating to form. Resilience asks us to bring the not-so-easy questions to the table: How can I grow from this? What is there to learn? And, one of my personal favorites, where is there wisdom here? This kind, curious, soft introspection moves us into a growth mindset. When this occurs, our life becomes the rich opportunity to practice and grow as a heart-based human being.

This growth mindset and strong determination to live a resilient life has given me endless motivation to face new challenges and suffering over the years. Knowing that there is a baseline of equanimity to fall back on and to find refuge in has allowed me to meet uncomfortable feelings and life's breakdowns with total trust and fearlessness. With upekkha we're no longer afraid of painful feelings and emotions. The ability to remain steadfast with our experience becomes more the default than despair or aversion. When we learn to stay with our failures, pain, and unpleasant feelings, even for just a split second, courage is born right there in the soft in-between of resilience and our old usual habitual patterns of coping.

Tonglen, from the Tibetan lineage of Buddhism, is a practice I teach specifically to grow inner strength and resilience as we find our way back to eventual balance and equanimity. In today's meditation I'll guide you through an adapted tonglen meditation to help you transform your pain and suffering into untapped inner strength and deeper understanding. With tonglen, you breathe in the suffering, pain, and hardship for yourself and others; and you breathe out the openness, relief, and wish for the alleviation of suffering. In our practice together today, you will breathe in all of the pain and difficulty you've been through, and breathe out the open possibility of learning and growth.

The brahma-viharas are meant to work intentionally with our feelings. They ask us to go *into* our feelings, instead of around them or in the opposite direction. Sometimes it's hard to accept difficult feelings and the painful things that happen to us or because of us. These divine qualities of the heart show us a way through. The heart gives us the necessary warmth, inner strength, and courage for the healing road of recovery and real resilience to emerge.

---

today's meditation

TONGLEN FOR INNER STRENGTH

- Allow yourself to settle into your meditation space.
- Make any movements needed to feel balanced, spacious, and at ease.
- As you feel ready, gently close your eyes and further settle your attention inward.
- Welcome yourself home to this moment and open yourself up to who you really are—a strong, boundless, and limitless being, open to learning from all that life has presented, no matter how pleasant or unpleasant, or anywhere in between.
- Let your attention softly scan your body.
- Bring this kind, warmhearted attention to your heart space and rest your awareness in the movements of the breath there.
- Sense your chest rising and falling, the muscles around your heart opening and closing, all in a perfect undefined rhythm, in symphony with the rhythms of life itself.

- Now we'll start our tonglen meditation for inner strength and transformation.
- On your inhale, imagine that you are breathing in all of the hardship and difficulty that you have gone through.
- At the top of this inhale, see if you can refrain from judging this difficulty you have endured and see if you can open to it, meeting it with eyes of equanimity and love.
- Then on your exhale, breathe out the relief and transmutation of this difficulty, with the authentic wish for you and others to find meaning and purpose with any of life's painful moments.
- Breathe in once again, inhaling all of the hardship and difficulty that you have gone through.
- See if you can meet this awareness of the past and any feelings held around it with the spaciousness of a vast limitless sky, a sky so many others have looked up to over the years to gain the strength and courage to overcome and stay steadfast with the experiences of their lives
- And breathe out, exhaling this shared humanity and this tender openheartedness that comes with the fearlessness and courage to choose strength and resilience.
- Keep breathing in with nonjudgment and wisdom, and breathing out with an inspired inner strength.
- Continue for as long as you'd like.
- When it comes time to bring this meditation to a close, rest your attention back in your heart space.
- With gratitude, thank your heart for its strength and resilience.
- When ready, open your eyes.

Pause for a moment, letting this meditation sink in. Then pick up your practice journal and go right into the following writing session.

REFLECTION QUESTION 1: What have some of my hardships taught me?

REFLECTION QUESTION 2: What is one of my resilient stories? (Think back to a time when you've experienced a setback or painful moment of some kind. How did you overcome that experience to be where you are today?)

REFLECTION QUESTION 3: How am I being resilient right now?

EQUANIMITY IN ACTION

Today's equanimity practice is to spend further time reflecting upon how your life experiences have led you to where you are right now. Resilience and strength ask us to meet life whole-heartedly. We don't turn away from the past. We turn toward it to teach us and give us the grace to move forward with more wisdom and understanding.

DAY 25

---

calm mind, calm heart

True nature is pure and deep
Like clear still water.
—Han Shan Te Ch'ing[27]

WHAT HAPPENS WHEN you simply rest your awareness in the heart of this moment? To begin your practice today, go ahead and see. Maybe you close your eyes for a moment and your attention just naturally settles in your heart space. Or perhaps it seems to suspend itself unconfined by time, hovering and floating openly and freely. Take in the texture of this present moment. Subtle impressions, much like a great van Gogh watercolor, move in and out of focus across your mind's eye. Right here, below, above, and all around the buzz of your daily thoughts and to-dos is the spacious stillness of the resting heart, a place unmoved and undisturbed by life's comings and goings and endless asks for your attention. Like the very bottom of an ocean or a great lake, there is an abiding peaceful awareness, a mind that is serene, open, tranquil, and at ease.

A taste of this spacious stillness can stir something deeply rooted inside of us. This calmness of heart and being has a reassuring feeling of the familiar and, simultaneously, an open-endedness of the vast unknown. As one of my meditation teacher friends likes to say, "It's like I know everything and nothing all at the same time." Or as I like to add, "It's the great knowing of 'don't-know mind,'" where everything is perceived as fresh and new, yet there is a deep trust present when we are in the curiosity of discovering what we know we don't know.

For some, equanimity can seem cerebral, conceptual, intellectual, or unattainable. For me, and as I have seen in others, to know equanimity is to feel it. It's a journey each one of us uniquely takes until we know it in our bones. This is how literal and practical equanimity can be. It is the foundation of the heart and the untouched inner stillness you can access at any time.

feel it to become it

Sometimes this evenness of mind or evenness of heart is easiest experienced when we actively visualize it during meditation. A teaching I really like in the Vedic tradition of meditation says there are four experiences you can have during your meditation practice: (1) the experience of your thoughts; (2) the object you are resting your attention on, such as a mantra or the breath; (3) the experience of falling asleep; (4) the experience of awareness itself, the space between your thoughts and between the concentration and effort that is required to keep your focused attention on the object of your attention. For a moment you may even think that you have fallen asleep, only at the same time you are aware that you haven't.

When I mention this fourth experience in my classes, I see eyes and faces light up: "What do you mean by the space *between* your thoughts?" or "Oh, that just happened to me in our meditation! I thought for a moment I might have fallen asleep, but I didn't . . . I was still sitting up and could tell I was awake." This fourth experience is marked by these kinds of experiences where the relaxed heart and the calm-abiding mind are resting in natural awareness. A meditation technique in the Buddhist tradition guides the practitioner to visualize this mind state so they can "see" it for themselves in order to feel it and then become it. Today I'll ask you to imagine a beautiful blue peaceful lake bordering the bottom of a strong earthly mountain. Especially for those of us who are visual thinkers or feel a little unsure of how to touch down into the inner stillness of equanimity we have within us, this meditation is a fantastic way to get to know the experience of surfing the surface waves of experience while tapping into the deeper waters of awareness and the spacious stillness in our very own mind and heart.

Ready? Let's begin.

today's meditation

CLEAR, PEACEFUL LAKE OF
EQUANIMITY MEDITATION

- To start, get nice and acclimated to today's meditation space and surroundings.
- When you are ready, close your eyes, feeling your two eyelids meet.
- Allow your attention to lightly rest in your body now, particularly noticing where your body is making contact with the seat and surface beneath you.
- Gently guide your attention back to the sensation of the breath, and keep a light background awareness of the breath as we begin today's visualization.

- In your mind's eye, start to see yourself approaching a glistening body of blue water. It is still off in the distance and you are walking toward it.
- Moving through the natural landscape, through the tall golden grasses, green meadows, and forested hillsides, the blue waters become clearer and closer.
- You start to see it is a clear blue lake resting at the bottom of a magnificent wise mountain.
- As you approach the sandy sides of this beautiful mountain lake, you see little ripples in the surface waters stirred by the winds of the north and the south.
- Then the winds calm and the lake becomes quiet and still in the golden setting afternoon sun.
- You peer downward into the calm, peaceful waters of the lake and you can start to see clearly into the lake's deeper waters.
- Here there are deeper hues of blue and the mirror image of the great mountain beside you.
- A calm-abiding tranquil feeling may arise in your heart.
- You feel calm and peaceful.
- Your mind is just like the quiet stillness of this beautiful blue mountain lake, undisturbed, serene, and still.
- Currents of life's wind will come and go, yet you know the deeper waters of your awareness are always residing in the same sweet stillness.
- Hold this image of your calm, clear lake of equanimity for the next several minutes in your mind.
- If your attention starts to wander from the lake to thoughts, refocus your attention back on your clear peaceful lake resting at the bottom of a magnificent mountain.
- When you're ready to bring this meditation to an end, allow the image of the mountain and lake to dissolve and gently open your eyes.

When you're ready, move right into your reflective journaling practice after this meditation. Stay in contact with any feelings or sensations of peace or ease or calmness as you pick up your pen and start writing about today's reflection questions.

REFLECTION QUESTION 1: What does it feel like when I am centered in my calm, relaxed awareness?
REFLECTION QUESTION 2: How does equanimity express itself to me?

EQUANIMITY IN ACTION

Equanimity can be felt directly. To access this feeling of equanimity, sometimes it may be easier to flash your mind to a visual image of equanimity. Look back to your answers and inner guidance from today's practice journal reflections and make a commitment to rest in equanimity three times during your day today. You may even want to take out your calendar and plan in these three moments of equanimity right now.

At the end of the day, think back to these three mini-moments of equanimity. Did you let your mind float back to the calm, peaceful lake of today's meditation or did something new come to mind? Did you simply feel more balanced and at ease when you allowed your heart to rest in its natural state of equanimity? There is no right or wrong way to access equanimity. Sometimes you must see, feel, and embody equanimity directly to become it.

———

DAY 26

---

this too shall pass

The world is always changing.
Learn how to allow for it.
—Elizabeth Gilbert

IT IS SAID THAT in the course of one lifetime, every single human being will experience every single emotion that there is. As you've come to know over these past few weeks, we are all bound to make contact with the ten thousand joys and ten thousand sorrows of being alive. In any given hour or minute, we can feel the sweetness of pleasure or the deflation of pain. When sitting in the middle of any moment with the wings of equanimity balancing your mind, you too can start to see the very nature of each emotion right before you. With this balanced view, you see the swirling, rising, dipping, pin-pricking, or happy-making *energy* behind each emotion you are in.

Emotions are energy in motion—energy being and behaving very similarly to the biochemical makeup of the natural world. What gives rise to a particle such as oxygen or gas can start out in a liquid form when the oxygen particle is bound to a molecule of hydrogen. This droplet of water may have even just thawed from its solid state of frozen icy lake top just met by the warmth of the morning sun as it lifts itself upward in the sky. Our emotional lives are subject to these very same laws of change, and so are our daily life experiences. This is universal truth: life is impermanent; whatever arises will change. Our work is to learn how to be with this changing world and our own shifting feelings.

it's okay to not be okay

The Buddha had a pretty glorious way of capturing this changing condition of our inner and outer lives. He called this the "the eight worldly vicissitudes," which really sums up the nature of reality itself. He said that we are all subject to the constantly changing conditions of gain and loss, praise and blame, fame and disrepute, and pleasure and pain. With equanimity we can see these fluctuations with more clarity and compassion. We can find grace amid the impermanence, and refuge within the wisdom—this too shall pass, *whatever* "this" may be.

At one point in my early meditation years, I thought I was doing something wrong if things weren't going my way or if I felt depressed or anxious. Sometimes I would bypass my feelings by not allowing myself to feel or stay with my sadness, worry, or fears. Instead, I would choose to "just think positively" or move right into strong aversion by literally ignoring my unpleasant emotions. I remember feeling like if I let myself sit in the loss or fear I was experiencing for too long, it would be like cracking open a lid to a whole Pandora's box of pain and despair. I see this same obstacle in many of my students when growing a meditation practice. Like me, they are afraid to sit with themselves, because the moment unpleasantness arises, it may feel like just too much to bear.

Through our mindfulness and heart practices, though, just like the inevitable changing of our emotional tides and conditions of our lives, eventually we aren't as afraid to keep our toes in the feelings of discomfort or pain. With trust and courage we place one foot down and even a fingertip and then a palm of our hand. And even though we are making direct contact with the pain of loss or criticism or a bruised ego or broken heart, it's in meeting our emotions around life's vicissitudes where the insight can arise: "This hurts. But I am still okay." We make an opening for the life-changing acknowledgment that it's okay to not be okay or feel okay at times.

Sometimes we fall and stumble into this insight of equanimity. I know I did. I had to develop a very basic trust and confidence in the fact that I wouldn't *always* get swallowed up by my own little Pandora's box of pain each and every time I dipped my toes into the reality of my discomfort. I soon discovered that even if I did get fully consumed by the emotion, it wasn't a permanent state as I feared. In fact, sometimes it was more fleeting than I could ever have imagined. Within a minute or two, the intensity, the overwhelm, the tears burning behind my eyelids would subside and fade into something else entirely on their own.

So much of our practice is mustering the courage to try out these principles for ourselves and see if they are indeed true. I encourage you to think back to a time when you thought the sorrow or happiness you were in would never end. For instance, I can think back to three distinct times when I was sure the stream of tears covering my face wouldn't end. It had already been hours, after all. In the same flash of recapitulation I can see three distinct chapters of my life where for several months I was so effortlessly happy and lighthearted. I specifically recall thinking with triumph and a lot of gratification, "This is it! I've made it. I'll probably never feel really bad again."

When looking at our own lives, we see this inevitable impermanence and constant state of flux and change mirroring back the very undercurrent of our existence: at some point this too will pass and as it does, we're going to be okay.

Building trust in this fundamental okayness takes time and a never-ceasing willingness to keep experimenting. Life will give you countless opportunities every single day to make your own testing ground and inner excavation site of upekkha. With each honest contact with your changing reality and the feelings surrounding it, you drill down a little deeper toward the wellspring of well-being and a fundamental okayness regardless of your internal and external circumstances. This is your baseline of equanimity. This is the trustworthy home within your heart and mind.

In today's meditation you will explore your feelings around trust, change, and the nature of reality—namely, that it is impermanent. If this feels a little intimidating, don't worry. I've got your back. I am here to remind you that your fundamental okayness is here for you.

---

today's meditation

LEARNING TO TRUST

- Take a comfortable seat in your meditation space and get psyched for today's practice.
- When you are ready, close your eyes.
- Breathe in and out deeply, inhaling through your nose and exhaling through your mouth.
- Let your breath settle naturally now.
- As you follow your natural breath, notice any passing sensations, thoughts, or feelings that may be here.

- Softly hold each with a clear and calm mind, watching the rising and falling away of thoughts, emotional undercurrents, or your body's signals of sensation.
- Then repeat in your mind:
  - This too shall pass. Right now or someday soon.
  - This too shall pass. Right now or someday soon.
- With mindfulness, keep noting your present moment experiences and apply this phrase.
- Now, lightly bring your attention back to the breath and with each breath warmly repeat these following phrases.

equanimity mantras

May I learn to see the rising and passing of all things with equanimity.
May I learn to be with things as they are.
May I meet each moment with balance and ease.
May I trust life's natural unfolding.

- Stay with these phrases for the remaining time in your meditation.
- End today's meditation with your hands over your heart space and by repeating the phrases, "May I feel calm and peaceful today. May I be at ease with the world and trust in life's natural flow and currents."
- Gently open your eyes.

Go ahead and take a moment to rest in this beautiful peace and ease you just grew! And take out your practice journal to get ready for a big spiritual assignment that will help you solidify your full month of heart practice.

LETTER TO YOUR FUTURE SELF

Today you will start a letter to your future self. Why your future self in the midst of a practice that beckons you to be as present as possible? In the words of my friend and meditation mentor Mark Coleman, "When you take care of this moment, the next present moments take care of themselves."[28] Mark's wisdom points us to a super-helpful principle about meditation: while the work we do now doesn't change the past, it can and does inform our future. You have created a new baseline of being and home from which to live from—that is, you're always with you, the unconditional mobile home of the heart. Your future you is already grateful for the time spent uprooting the obstructions to boundless love in your heart and mind. Your future you is looking upon you now with the loving heart and mind you are embodying today. This letter is just for you, though you may want to share it with a close loved one or confidant. It will be both a way to integrate your insights from your four weeks of practice surrounding the brahma-viharas and a way to remind your future self of all the learnings and wisdom you've uncovered.

Spend a few moments before you begin reflecting upon what this month of practice has meant to you and the shifts, major to minor, you've already seen come to fruition! And since no one knows you better than you, think ahead to what your future self might find helpful to hear and what it is precisely about metta, karuna, mudita, and upekkha that you'd like to keep top of mind and heart as you move forward.

Here are some guiding questions you can freewrite on:

- Moving forward, I want to remember . . .
- How do I want to continue living from a loving heart and mind?

- What may I forget that I want to keep top of mind and heart?
- What have been some of my most moving insights and realizations from practicing with the brahma-viharas?
- What are some ways to come back home to an open heart?
- What are commitments and steps I can make to live my most authentic and intentional life?
- How do I want to take care of this moment in order to take care of my future self?

Don't worry if you feel as though this letter may take a bit of time for you to write and reflect about! Tomorrow's daily practice is to finish any part of this letter you want to have more time with. Write your heart out on these pages. This is how you bravely live your practice one day at a time.

EQUANIMITY IN ACTION

Equanimity is not the same as indifference. It is not a place of "everything is fine, it doesn't matter, it's all impermanent anyway." Equanimity is holding our life moment to moment, with great care, openness, and trust in our ability to be with our changing experiences wholeheartedly.

Today, notice where you can open fully to the changing nature of your feelings, thoughts, and circumstances and how holding this understanding of impermanence asks you to find a wild amount of faith and trust in your heart. Also repeat this mantra as needed: "It's alright, dear one, this too shall pass."

———

DAY 27

---

inner freedom

The words liberation, compassion, love, and
wisdom fell like drops of medicine on my heart.
—Zenju Earthlyn Manuel

YOUR INNERMOST FREEDOM can be found in a heart that holds just the right balance between boundless love and wisdom. To cultivate this open, balanced awareness, one that flows with the parameters of authentic ethics and moral guidance, alongside a love that knows no limits, today we will settle into the teachings on how to move beyond craving and aversion, two states of the mind that can arrest our heart's innate state of liberation.

On Day 22, our first day of upekkha practice, you began to decipher the fundamental feeling tones of daily experience, and yesterday, Day 26, you meditated on the changing nature of this daily existence. These are such insightful teachings into what it means to be living a human life, especially during present times. Until we get a glimpse of these truths of reality, it's like walking through life as if we're fumbling around in a dimly lit room. The teachings turn on the lamp of awareness. All of a sudden, we can see what to do more clearly and with greater conviction.

craving and aversion

Identifying whether any given moment is pleasant, unpleasant, or neutral gives us the purview into our present relationship with pleasure, pain, or the neutrality that can be found in between. For instance, a moment of pleasantness where we feel pleasure, happiness, or joyous bliss usually forms a strong feeling of craving and attachment to the pleasantness that we are feeling. We never want the pleasure of pleasantness to go away. We become enthralled with and attached to always feeling pleasant and we crave it in a very deep way.

With a moment of unpleasantness, as you may imagine, the opposite transpires. When we encounter discomfort, pain, unhappiness, or anything we don't like, right on the heels of this dissatisfaction arises a strong aversion or pushing away of our experience. We may even label the experience as "bad" and shut down our heart in the face of uncomfortableness. Most of us teeter between these two extremes. Pain makes us run right into pleasure. When the pleasure ends, we immediately feel in pain.

Then there is our reaction to a neutral experience, that space when we are just sitting on the couch, not necessarily in a high moment of pleasantness or in the acute awareness of not liking what is happening, and we find ourselves checking out into inattentiveness by flipping on a movie or the news, grabbing for our phone, or feeling sleepy. We may even chalk up that moment of neutrality to boredom.

As you read this, you may be feeling a bit of familiarity with your own experience of craving and aversion. Or you may be thinking, "This is no way to live! How dissatisfying." Don't sweat it. Having a balanced, wise view of these three flavor tones of experience and our usual way of reacting to them becomes the path to real inner freedom. With the wisdom of nonreactivity found in the practice of equanimity, we can liberate ourselves from this wheel of suffering. You, too, can achieve the freedom of heart and liberation of an open, balanced awareness.

liberation now

I find these practices of inner freedom to be so fun. That's right—fun, because we can free ourselves from habitual unawake reactions. To do this, we step into the craving mind and all of the feelings of attachment to pleasure and meet ourselves fully with the applications of kindness and compassion. Equally, we can look at what it feels like to turn our back on pain and any hint of discomfort with kindness and compassion. Holding this with the balanced view of nonreactivity—"Ah, craving is like this. Ah, aversion is like that. May I hold this too with compassion. May I hold this too in a balanced view and with kindness."—gives us the keys to our inner freedom. We see things, others, and ourselves as we are given the opportunity to choose the path of openheartedness. It is through the heart and the clear view of reality that we can find our way to liberation.

Today's meditation will be a classic metta-meets-mindfulness practice where I'll guide you in seeing things as they are and then applying the transformational qualities of the heart. Ready? Let's get started!

---

today's meditation

SEEING THINGS AS THEY
ARE LIBERATION MEDITATION

- Spend a few moments getting nice and set up for your meditation.
- When you're ready, gently close your eyes.

- Guide your attention to the sensation of the breath at first, then expand your awareness to your full body.
- You may notice the feeling of your body being supported and held by the earth below it.
- Give yourself a moment to rest in this supportive feeling of being cared for.
- Guide your attention back to sensations of the breath.
- Each time you become aware of a thought, sound, or feeling and sensation in the body, note it as pleasant, unpleasant, or neutral.
- If pleasant, see if there is any clinging or grasping to the pleasant feeling.
- If unpleasant, see if there is any aversion to the unpleasant feeling and sensations.
- If neutral, notice your relationship to neutrality. Do you want something pleasant to take its place, or do you want to label neutrality as boredom?
- Now silently say to yourself the following mantras.

equanimity mantras

This is just how it is right now.
May I understand things as they are and meet my
life through the eyes of freedom and love.

- Repeat this three times.
- Take a deep breath and softly open your eyes.

Following today's meditation, move right into your reflection practice. Pick up your practice journal and pen and start writing down any insights on the following questions.

REFLECTION QUESTION 1: Where may I feel caught in craving or aversion? How can I meet this with kindness and compassion?

REFLECTION QUESTION 2: What does liberation and freedom mean to me? How can I live in my full authentic expression of liberation now?

Let your hand freely capture your thoughts on the page. When you are done, pause, take a breath, and feel into the inner freedom you just gained today!

EQUANIMITY IN ACTION

At some point during your day today finish your letter to your future self that you started on Day 26. You may want to do this right now or a little before bedtime as part of your evening wind-down routine. As you'll discover tomorrow, this letter is going to be not only something you can look back to in the future to remind yourself of all your insights and aspirations from this month of heart practice. It will also serve as a key supportive ingredient for the life-changing practice you will experience tomorrow as part of our closing celebration of your choice to make a loving and heavenly home in your heart.

———

DAY 28

——

open-hearted living

We are not just humans learning to become
buddhas, but also buddhas waking up in human
form, learning to become fully human.
—John Welwood

TODAY IS THE LAST DAY of your twenty-eight-day journey of the heart. Welcome to your new home within the heart and your newfound inner wisdom, authenticity, and deepened meditation practice! In many ways today is not only a day to celebrate the great voyage and all of the heart work you have done but also a day of stepping into your new way of being and living. In essence you have developed your capacity to live your life with an open mind and heart. This, my friend, is no small feat.

Throughout many ancient wisdom traditions, days like today are witnessed by some kind of ceremonial rite of passage, an inner and outer celebration of honoring the metamorphosis, real change, and new beginnings of the individual. These ceremonial celebrations mark transitions from what is known to what is new; a letting go of the past and a stepping into the future with new inner means and resources, and with newfound eyes of wisdom and compassion in which to view the world.

These teachings of the heart are meant to ripen over time. In my own heart journey, I have found this to be indisputably true. Some Buddhist texts say that by just hearing the Buddha's teachings, some of his students immediately became enlightened. Others start the lifelong practice of tending to the seeds of love and awakening instilled in them after receiving the truth of loving awareness and wisdom in the Buddha's words. At this very moment, I can think back to teachings I heard five years ago that just sparked a revelation today. The reason being that today gave me a new and different opportunity to practice with that exact technique, teaching, and application of the heart and mind. I was given the opportunity to step deeper into right action by speaking up with a family member who held a different view than mine. I forgave someone I thought I wouldn't or couldn't ever forgive and now they have become someone who, through our friendship, continues to encourage me to soften into the fierce tenderness I know now to be a part of any authentic code.

Our teachings and tools of practice become like flowering herbs in a meadow: we pick the exact herb on the precise day that holds the very medicine within its flowers, leaves, buds, and stems we need as a remedy. Living in this way allows for life to become the practice field and the practice—how we live our lives.

The gift of the brahma-viharas is to be of the world and yet not overwhelmed by the suffering we see or endure. The heart points us to the hope and capacity of a boundless humanitarian love, recognizing within our differences there is still oneness, which is the wish to be free and happy. We live from the open-heartedness of this truth: "Just like me, you want to be happy. Just like you, I too want to be loved and free." We each aspire to be the best version of ourself, and we are doing it the best we know how, one messy human moment at a time.

In the *Metta Sutta*, the Buddha spoke of openheartedness, love, and metta.

He said,

So with a boundless heart
Should one cherish all living beings;
Radiating kindness over the entire world:
Spreading upward to the skies,
And downward to the depths;
Outwards and unbounded,
Freed from hatred and ill-will.
Whether standing or walking, seated or lying down
Free from drowsiness,
One should sustain this recollection.
This is said to be the sublime abiding.[29]

So this is the home we choose to build and stand in. This is the home we welcome our lived experiences into. Regardless of what position or situation you are in, you can always decide to choose kindness now. When you live from this place of love, each person becomes your teacher. Nothing is missed as an opportunity to practice becoming more authentically you: who you are, what you stand for, and what you know to be your dharma as unique as your own breath and pulsing heart. This, my dear reader and fellow truth seeker, is where the awakened heart of awareness becomes your new abiding. Each of us as meditators and conduits of loving compassion form our own version of this credo. Living with this bigheartedness becomes the expression of your commitment to metta, karuna, mudita, and upekkha manifesting into being through your presence, words, and actions.

celebrate your heart work!

Though your new chapter of openhearted living is just beginning, today we will celebrate the culmination of your heart studies by going through our own ceremonial mini-rite of passage. In today's meditation you will imagine a circle of benefactors, those whom you love and who have automatic metta and mudita for you, and those who inspire you to no end and are your guides on this path of living from the heart. Maybe Nelson Mandela is in your circle, or Thich Nhat Hanh or Quan Yin. Maybe a teacher you have learned from before is in this circle, or someone who's book you've read that has been a part of your practice path; or your ancestors, your great-grandmother, your grandfather, or a loved one. You better believe, without a doubt, that I'll be there in your circle of benefactors today. I am honored at the work you have done and equally honored to be walking this path of the heart together.

After imagining your circle of benefactors, you'll send out wishes of equanimity to all beings everywhere, just like you have practiced over the past four weeks of uncovering your heart's unconditional love. You'll cultivate equal loving-kindness for all beings, equal compassion for all beings, and equal appreciative joy for all beings, all with the profound aspiration that all beings everywhere may know equanimity in their hearts—if not today, then someday soon.

Before your meditation practice today, see if there is any outward expression you'd like to make for your ceremonial celebration. Is there an object or two you'd like with you to encapsulate the energy of this special moment? Or some flowers or candles you'd like to gather, or a note you'd like to jot down and have in front of you during your meditation? If you'd like to go and get your letter to your future self and place it by your side for your celebration meditation, you can do so now. Take a minute to metta-fy your space and fill it with the love emanating from within you. Then when you're ready, let's begin.

today's meditation

ARRIVING HOME TO YOUR
OPEN HEART MEDITATION

- With joy and appreciation, settle into your practice space for today's meditation.
- Take a few deep breaths and close your eyes.
- For a moment, rest your awareness in your body, softening your body, inviting in love and kindness.
- Guide your attention to your heart space now, noticing the rise and fall of the breath and the natural expression of life itself always present within your breathing.
- Begin to visualize your ceremonial celebration circle of benefactors here to witness you on this last day of your *Kindness Now* journey. With love and wisdom in their eyes, they too know that today is actually just the beginning.
- Spend a moment resting in each of your benefactor's field of happiness and radiating warmth. See each of them as if they are right here with you.
- The happiness in their hearts sparks joy within yours.
- They are here to witness you as you arrive home to your open compassionate heart and new way of living.
- With their presence all around you, take a deep breath in and a deep breath out.
- Now, start to silently wish the following mantras of equanimity to all beings, in all directions around you, everywhere.

equanimity mantras

May all beings know the truth of equanimity
    and peace.
May all beings' happiness never cease.
May all beings feel at ease in the world.
May all beings find a home of love in their hearts.

- Repeat these wishes of love and equanimity for as long as you'd like.
- Notice your heart grow and expand with each repetition of the mantras.
- When you're ready, let the mantras fade away.
- Bring back your circle of benefactors into your mind's eye.
- With your awareness in and around your heart, bow to them and see them bowing back to you.
- When you are ready, open your eyes.

Rest for a moment in the stillness and magnitude of your practice. Allow yourself to take in this moment of transition and culmination all within this present moment. Rejoice in your past twenty-eight days of heart practice and get psyched to now move forward with all of the wisdom that has been gained.

YOUR *KINDNESS NOW* VOW

Today's writing in your practice journal is to sketch down a simple statement that encompasses your commitments moving forward. You can read the letter you've written over the past two days or just allow whatever is here to flow through you. This can be a vow to keep living from an open heart or practicing compassion whenever you can. This can be to embody kindness and love now, or to live a life of nonharm. Take the next few moments coming up with your credo, your heart statement, your mantra of openheartedness, your vow that you can carry with you from this day forward.

After you've written down your heart credo, place your hands over your heart and silently repeat it three times in your mind. Soak it up and in, rest in the boundless potential and love within this promise and heart-based declaration. You've just made a vow to live your kindness now.

EQUANIMITY IN ACTION

Your daily practice today is to repeat your *Kindness Now* Vow over and over throughout the day. Or at least at three different times with intention. You'll always have this mantra now to help you sustain this recollection and stay rooted in this sublime abiding. Even though today is Day 28 and your month of heart practice is now a part of who you are, in many ways these teachings will continue to grow, deepen, and ripen inside of you. All of these seeds of aspiration you have been planting are now on their way to full bloom. In the following conclusion, I'll share some ways to stay connected to your heart home and keep these teachings alive.

————

CONCLUSION

BECOMING YOUR LOVE

Love is always the place
where I begin and end.
—bell hooks

The biggest work we can do in our lifetimes is turning over our small-mindedness to vast bigheartedness and to live our lives as close to the heart as humanly possible. Here, we assume the authenticity we were born with. We discover the heart's intuitive wisdom rooted in the timeless abiding of loving awareness that, while messy at times, is always working on our behalf and toward the greatest good for all. Being heart-based, we let our lives become the living expression of the heart's unconditional way of responding with ardent solidarity, nonharm, and compassion. Through the heart practices we become the embodiment of living with a mind of love. It is here, your chitta becomes *bodhichitta*, the awakened mind and heart that know how to respond in service to love.

The Buddhist meditation teacher Dipa Ma is known as the "patron saint of householders." To this day, a rare matriarch in the monastic lineages of Buddhism often comprising mainly men, she held the fierce conviction that anyone could wake up, that anyone could attain enlightenment, and yet more practically, that anyone could practice mindfulness and metta no matter what their lives looked like. One time a student asked her whether regular daily life was different from meditation. Her response? "You cannot separate meditation from life."[30] Practice and life are not separate or two different things. In other words, life is practice and practice is life.

Dipa Ma was also a firm believer that there was no separation between mindfulness and loving-kindness. What she practiced with great passion became a presence infused with boundless, limitless love. Just walking into a room with her, students would immediately recognize a palpable field of love and the call to slow down into the present moment. In 1984, Dipa Ma was leaving the Insight Meditation Society in Barre, Massachusetts, circled by a group of teachers and students all there to wish her farewell and safe travels by holding their hands in a bow of prayer and salutation at their heart centers. Right as Dipa Ma was about to step into the van to leave, she paused and took one of the student's hands still being held in a bow at her heart and held them in her own two hands. She looked the student in the eyes and held her hands in noble silence for a full minute and gave her a gift only found in the heart—a direct unspoken transmission of loving-kindness. After, the student said it was a kind of love she had never experienced before, one without boundaries, attachment, force, or hindrance, and free from all segregation or difference. Dipa Ma was indeed a living example of being a lamp of love. Just by being near her you would receive a transmission of belonging and refuge, care and unconditional concern, all stemming from the unshakable love and dwelling of her heart home.

One of the most common questions I get asked about the heart practices is, "How do I know if it's even working if it feels like I'm just going through the motions, or repeating words without really meaning them, or feeling, well, even half-hearted about the practice?" As in Dipa Ma's way of teaching, by being the living example of love and living the practice as though there's no divide between the mind and heart. I often tell students that just by following through on the intention to practice metta, karuna, mudita, and upekkha, even when it feels awkward, utterly forced, or mechanical, you are unveiling your bodhichitta—one aspirational phrase and one intentional heart-minded response at a time.

to know kindness

The heart practices are medicine for the heart. They will turn your suffering into service, your pain into purpose, your brokenness into belonging, and your perceived separation into connection. To undergo the month of heart practice to which you just dedicated yourself means you just trained your muscle of kindness and built your inner abode, your refuge, your true home out of real love. You have boldly chosen the way of kindness and the path of the heart, one committed to transforming your personal suffering into the fertile soil of potentiality and healing. You have become chitta-fyed and metta-fyed. You have now walked through the passage into bodhichitta—you are awake and aware in the world with a mind made of love. And whether it feels like it right now or not, you have also taken a stand for loving-kindness, the equity of radical inclusion, and the fearlessness of seeing every other being through the eyes of kindness and compassion, not as separate or apart from you. Most of all, you have become a living, breathing example of living a profound emboldened love, one without limits or boundaries. You have learned how to live with kindness now. What an awesome responsibility.

on staying heart-based

The inner work you've done over these past twenty-eight days is one of bigheartedness, true love, and the deep-seated excavation of fear and separation. You've made yourself safe enough to be a refuge for others and to offer your heart medicine as you walk alongside them. The real radical news, too, is you've also deepened your daily meditation habit! You've traversed the landscape of both your mind's true nature and the innate goodness of your heart. Though Day 28 is now complete, your heart work has really just begun. Moving forward, the path of the heart is not linear, nor will it always make sense to the thinking mind. Therefore I want you to have a few tools to move forward with. After all, as you've discovered, to be heart-based and a human fully dedicated to meeting each opportunity life gives you with kindness, compassion, appreciate joy, and equanimity, means doing the work of the moment. This is actually what this moment in time and the world are requiring of us, bodhisattvas and heart-based humans. So here's my guidance on how to keep living your love after today.

HOW TO STAY GROUNDED IN YOUR NEW ABODE

1. **STAY PRACTICED.** If there is anything I want to encourage you to do moving forward it's to keep up with your daily meditation practice and sadhana (spiritual practice) routine. This is essential. To keep uncovering the innate healing potential of unconditional love and kindness, and practicing with the four pillars of love, let your entire life become the practice of living from the heart. And maintain your heart's foundation and four walls of love by spending time in your own reservoir of sacred stillness each and every day. Whatever routine you have established, stay with it, nurture it, love

it up, and stay committed to it. Keep journaling, reflecting, and meditating. Remember, you can return to these pages and meditations anytime that you need to.

2. MAKE IT SIMPLE—*BE KIND*. Nyoshul Khen Rinpoche, a great Dzogchen master, says it simply like this: "I would like to pass on one little bit of advice I give everyone. Relax, just relax. Be nice to each other. As you go through life, simply be kind to people. Try to help them rather than hurt them. Try to get along with them, rather than fall out with them. With that, I will leave you, and with all my very best wishes."[31] In the same relaxed simplicity, recall the three ways of kindness you have been exploring over the past twenty-eight days. We learn the way of kindness by:

- being on the receiving end of kindness from others,
- learning to extend kindness to ourselves, and
- giving kindness to others.

Each of the brahma-viharas are communicated and expressed through these three vehicles of kindness. So if ever you are in doubt of how to come in contact with and communicate your deepest heart's intentions and intrinsic good-heartedness, choose one of the vehicles above, express your kindness in that way and let it be that simple.

3. YOU CAN ALWAYS COME BACK HOME. In the same way you are always one breath away from the present moment, you are always one moment away from remembering your true nature and metta-fyed home base in the heart. You've learned that love is a choice, and to return to love is also always a choice. My suggestion from this day onward is to find your unique ways and entry points to coming back home to your heart center. Be it meditation, a mindful walk, a moment of stillness, an actual day away from the inbox or your work, a

mindful cup of coffee or tea, or your favorite music tune to get lost in, remember your unique authentic code to finding your way home to your heart's loving abode.

Be unapologetically full of any and all of the feels right now. You have just undergone a life-changing training on love and living from the heart. I am so proud of your courage, strength, and resilience. I am honored to have been a part of your last month of making your heart a loving unconditional radiant home. No matter how you may feel right now, know that just by planting the seeds of love in your heart and mind, your beautiful garden of practice will bloom exactly at the right time. Continue to let your heart lead and know your authentic intentions will have your back each breath and step of the way moving forward. Know that each practice you have learned is now supporting you in living tenderly and fiercely with a love-filled mind and an open awakened heart.

Now, keep practicing kindness now.

ACKNOWLEDGMENTS

I first want to thank you, my dear reader. Knowing these pages would one day be in your hands was the very motivation that guided my writing and my own heart traversing. This book called me into the deepest layers of authenticity and intention, and at its conclusion I found the words and teachings had changed me from the inside out. My hope is that it shares the same transformational magic with you and that it touches your heart and mind, as it has mine.

This book would not have come into being without the generous support of a considerable amount of people and my beloved teachers. I owe a mountain of gratitude to those who were unconditionally enthusiastic about this book project from inception to fruition, including Adreanna Limbach, Lodro Rinzler, and Beth Frankl. The three of you have been my literary guides and base of compassionate encouragement during each step of this book's creation—thank you. I am deeply grateful to Shambhala Publications for welcoming me and my book into your lineage of authors and titles. Thank you for your vision and support. It has been a dream to work with you.

I would like to thank my sister Jordan Gilbert for being my lionhearted reader during the writing process and for challenging me to stretch and grow into who I needed to be for this book. Your unwavering support has meant the world. To Galit Szolomowicz, thank you for your encouragement and moral support during each step of the writing journey. I am endlessly grateful to my teachers and the lineage of meditation traditions I have trained in. Without you, I would not have these teachings to share. To Diana Winston, Dr. Marvin Belzer, Matthew Brensilver, Mark Coleman, Trudy Goodman, Jack Kornfield, and Dr. Deepak Chopra—thank you for your mentorship and teachings. I have boundless gratitude for my mentor, Dr. Elissa Epel. Elissa, thank you for showing me what heart-based leadership looks like, and for your continued support over the years. To Dr. Clifford Saron, thank you for sharing your story and dedicated practice with us in these pages.

To my mother, Sharon Gilbert, thank you for always asking how the book was coming along and for being my greatest supporter in my life. To Scott Gilbert, Kelan Gilbert, Marilyn Gilbert, Palmer Quaroni, and Robert Alpaugh (in loving memory), thank you for always supporting me.

I also want to thank the land and people of Topanga, California, where this book was written in 2020. Your kindness is infused into each word written on these pages. And to my students, whose practice has lent to the stories and composite stories found within each day's teachings. Thank you for sharing your heart and practice with me. May your dedication to truth and loving awareness continue to grow and inspire others in their journey home to the heart.

NOTES

1. "Karaniya Metta Sutta: The Buddha's Words on Loving-Kindness" (Sn 1.8), translated from the Pali by the Amaravati Sangha. *Access to Insight (BCBS Edition)*, November 2, 2013, www.accesstoinsight.org/tipitaka/kn/snp/snp.1.08. amar.html.
2. Sharon Salzberg, *The Kindness Handbook: A Practical Companion* (Boulder, CO: Sounds True, 2008), 22.
3. Jack Kornfield and Gil Fronsdal, eds., *Teachings on the Buddha* (Boston: Shambhala Publications, 1996), 135–36.
4. Viktor E. Frankl, *Man's Search for Meaning* (Boston: Beacon Press, 2014), 106.
5. Chögyam Trungpa, *The Bodhisattva Path of Wisdom and Compassion* (Boulder, CO: Shambhala Publications, 2013), 16.
6. Sharon Salzberg, *Lovingkindness: The Revolutionary Art of Happiness* (Boulder, CO: Shambhala Publications, 1995), 25.
7. Pema Chödrön, *The Places That Scare You: A Guide to Fearlessness in Difficult Times* (Boston, MA: Shambhala Publication, 2001), 42.
8. Chögyam Trungpa, *The Bodhisattva Path of Wisdom and Compassion* (Boulder, CO: Shambhala Publications, 2013), 16.

9. "Karaniya Metta Sutta: The Buddha's Words on Loving-Kindness," (Sn 1.8), translated from the Pali by The Amaravati Sangha. *Access to Insight (BCBS Edition)*, November 2, 2013, www.accesstoinsight.org/tipitaka/kn/snp/snp.1.08.amar.html.

10. Christopher K. Germer, *The Mindful Path to Self-Compassion: Freeing Yourself from Destructive Thoughts and Emotions* (New York: Guilford Press, 2009), 32.

11. Tom Moon, "Four Liberating Questions," The Work of Byron Katie, accessed November 23, 2020, https://thework.com/2017/10/four-liberating-questions.

12. Mark Coleman, "Mindfulness as a Path of Awakening" (retreat, Spirit Rock Meditation Center, Woodacre, CA, November 26–December 2, 2018).

13. His Holiness the 14th Dalai Lama, "Shantideva's Bodhisattva Vow," in *The Wise Heart: A Guide to the Universal Teachings of Buddhist Psychology*, by Jack Kornfield (New York: Bantam Books, 2008), 355.

14. Thich Nhat Hanh, *Teachings on Love* (Berkeley, CA: Parallax Press, 2007), 8.

15. Jonathan Haidt, "The Positive Emotion of Elevation," *Prevention and Treatment* 3, no. 1 (March 2000): doi.org/10.1037/1522-3736.3.1.33c.

16. Paul Ekman, *Emotions Revealed: Recognizing Faces and Feelings to Improve Communication and Emotional Life*, 2nd ed. (New York: Henry Holt, 2003), 190–99.

17. Matthieu Ricard, *Happiness: A Guide to Developing Life's Most Important Skill* (New York: Hachette Book Group, 2003), 44.

18. His Holiness the Dalai Lama and Desmond Tutu, with Douglas Abrams, *The Book of Joy: Lasting Happiness in a Changing World* (New York: Avery, 2016), 53.

19. Dalai Lama and Tutu, *Book of Joy*, 48.

20. Hidehiko Takahashi, Motoichiro Kato, Masato Matsuura, Dean Mobbs, Tetsuya Suhara, and Yoshiro Okubo, "When Your Gain Is My Pain and Your Pain Is My Gain: Neural Correlates of Envy and Schadenfreude," *Science* 323, no. 5916, (February 13, 2009): 937–39, science.sciencemag.org/content/323/5916/937.abstract.

21. Alex M. Wood, Stephen Joseph, and John Maltby, "Gratitude Predicts Psychological Well-Being Above the Big Five Facets," *Personality and Individual Differences* 46, no. 4 (2009): 443–47, http://citeseerx.ist.psu.edu/viewdoc/download?doi=10.1.1.606.6025&rep=rep1&type=pdf.

22. Shantideva, *The Way of the Bodhisattva*, trans. the Padmakara Translation Group (Boston: Shambhala, 1997), 166.

23. Amanda Gilbert, "Finding the Doorway to Meditation Practice," interview by David London, *Deskbound Therapy Podcast*, Ep. 24. April 17, 2020, Audio, 56:53, https://podcasts.apple.com/us/podcast/ep-24-finding-doorway-to-meditation-practice-ft-amanda/id1416804153?i=1000475733347.

24. Dalai Lama and Tutu, *Book of Joy*, 263.

25. Matthieu Ricard, *On the Path to Enlightenment: Heart Advice from the Great Tibetan Masters* (Boulder, CO: Shambhala Publications, 2013), 77.

26. Pema Chödrön, *When Things Fall Apart* (Boulder, CO: Shambhala Publications, 1997), 143–44.

27. Han Shan Te Ch'ing, *The Poetry of Enlightenment: Poems by Ancient Chan Masters*, trans. Chan Master Sheng Yen (Boston: Shambhala Publications, 1987), 99.

28. Mark Coleman, "Mindfulness As a Path of Awakening" (retreat, Spirit Rock Meditation Center, Woodacre, CA, November 26–December 2, 2018).

29. "Karaṇīya Metta Sutta: The Buddha's Words on Loving-Kindness" (Sn 1.8), translated from the Pali by the Amaravati Sangha. *Access to Insight (BCBS Edition)*, November 2, 2013, www.accesstoinsight.org/tipitaka/kn/snp/snp.1.08.amar.html.

30. Amy Schmidt, *Dipa Ma: The Life and Legacy of a Buddhist Master* (Katonah, NY: BlueBridge, 2005), 42.

31. Joseph Goldstein, *Mindfulness: A Practical Guide to Awakening* (Boulder, CO: Sounds True, 2013), 358.

VERSE CREDITS

Page 132: His Holiness the 14th Dalai Lama's interpretation of the Bodhisattva Prayer from Shantideva. Reprinted with permission.

Page 171: Excerpt from Shantideva, *The Way of the Bodhisattva*, trans. the Padmakara Translation Group (Boston: Shambhala, 1997), 166. Reprinted with permission.

Page 215: Excerpt from Han Shan Te Ch'ing, *The Poetry of Enlightenment: Poems by Ancient Chan Masters*, trans. Chan Master Sheng Yen (Boston: Shambhala Publications, 1987), location 1083. Reprinted with permission.

Page 237: *Metta Sutta* excerpt from "Karaniya Metta Sutta: The Buddha's Words on Loving-Kindness" (Sn 1.8), translated from the Pali by the Amaravati Sangha. *Access to Insight (BCBS Edition)*, November 2, 2013, www.accesstoinsight.org/tipitaka/kn/snp/snp.1.08. amar.html. ©1994 English Sangha Trust. You may copy, reformat, reprint, republish, and redistribute this work in any medium whatsoever, provided that: (1) you only make such copies, etc. available *free of charge*; (2) you clearly indicate that any derivatives of this work (including translations) are derived

ABOUT THE AUTHOR

Amanda Gilbert is a meditation teacher, lecturer of mindfulness at the University of Southern California, speaker, and author. She has been a meditator for over seventeen years and now leads meditation for top companies like NBC, Paramount Pictures, W Hotels, Merrill Lynch, Macy's, and YouTube. Before dedicating herself to teaching full-time, Amanda was the center director for the Aging, Metabolism, and Emotions Center at the University of California, San Francisco, a world-renowned health psychology laboratory conducting scientific research and publishing investigations on the biological and psychological effects of mindfulness, meditation, and stress resilience. Her formal meditation training has been with UCLA's Mindful Awareness Research Center, in primordial sound meditation with Deepak Chopra, and in the Insight Meditation tradition. She is now a modern leader in the field of teaching secular meditation, mindfulness, and Buddhist meditation.

www.amandagilbertmeditation.com